STRIVING LESS
AND TRUSTING
GOD MORE

Isaiah

MELISSA SPOELSTRA

Lifeway Press®
Brentwood, Tennessee

Published by Lifeway Press® • © 2022 Melissa Spoelstra
Reprinted March 2023

ISBN: 978-1-0877-5095-8 • Item: 005834277
Dewey decimal classification: 224.1
Subject headings: TRUST / BIBLE. O.T. ISAIAH—STUDY AND TEACHING / GOD—WILL

Unless indicated otherwise, all Scripture quotations are taken from the Holy Bible, New Living Translation, copyright ©1996, 2004, 2007, 2013, 2015 by Tyndale House Foundation. Used by permission of Tyndale House Publishers, Inc., Carol Stream, IL 60188. All rights reserved. Scripture marked ESV is taken from The ESV® Bible (The Holy Bible, English Standard Version®) copyright © 2001 by Crossway, a publishing ministry of Good News Publishers. ESV® Text Edition: 2011. All rights reserved. Scripture marked NIV is taken from the THE HOLY BIBLE, NEW INTERNATIONAL VERSION®, NIV® Copyright © 1973, 1978, 1984 by Biblica, Inc.® Used by permission. All rights reserved worldwide. Scripture marked CSB is taken from the Christian Standard Bible®, Copyright © 2017 by Holman Bible Publishers. Used by permission. Christian Standard Bible® and CSB® are federally registered trademarks of Holman Bible Publishers. Scripture marked NASB are taken from the New American Standard Bible® (NASB), Copyright © 1960, 1962, 1963, 1968, 1971, 1972, 1973, 1975, 1977, 1995 by The Lockman Foundation. Used by permission. www.lockman.org. Scripture marked NKJV are taken from the New King James Version®. Copyright © 1982 by Thomas Nelson. Used by permission. All rights reserved.

To order additional copies of this resource, write to Lifeway Resources Customer Service; 200 Powell Place, Suite 100; Brentwood, TN 37027-7707; order online at www.lifeway.com; fax 615.251.5933; phone toll free 800.458.2772; or email orderentry@lifeway.com.

Printed in the United States of America

Lifeway Women Bible Studies • Lifeway Resources
• 200 Powell Place, Suite 100 • Brentwood, TN 37027-7707

Cover design by Lauren Ervin

EDITORIAL TEAM, LIFEWAY WOMEN BIBLE STUDIES

Becky Loyd
Director, Lifeway Women

Tina Boesch
Manager

Chelsea Waack
Production Leader

Laura Magness
Content Editor

Lindsey Bush
Production Editor

Lauren Ervin
Art Director

Sarah Hobbs
Graphic Designer

Contents

ABOUT THE AUTHOR

Melissa Spoelstra is a women's conference speaker, Bible teacher, and author who is madly in love with Jesus. She is passionate about studying God's Word and helping women of all ages to seek Christ and know Him more intimately through serious Bible study. Melissa has a degree in Bible theology, and she enjoys teaching God's Word to the body of Christ, traveling to diverse groups and churches across the nation.

Melissa is the author of many Bible studies, including *Acts: Awakening to God in Everyday Life* and *The Names of God: His Character Revealed.*
She has also authored several books, including *Dare to Hope* and *Total Family Makeover: 8 Practical Steps to Making Disciples at Home.* She is a regular contributor to the Proverbs 31 First Five App, the Girlfriends in God online daily devotional, and many magazines and blogs. Melissa enjoys spending time with her pastor husband, Sean, and their four adult children: Zach, Abby, Sara, and Rachel.

DEDICATION

This Bible study is dedicated to the pastors who taught God's Word to me with clarity and passion during my childhood and teenage years:

Pastor Reggie McNeal
Pastor Mike Kessler
Brother Nick Harris

I'm so grateful for your teaching. It made me hungry for more of God through the study of His Word and helped me learn to strive less and trust God more!

FOLLOW MELISSA

Twitter	@MelSpoelstra
Instagram	@Melissa.Spoelstra
Facebook	/AuthorMelissaSpoelstra
Website	MelissaSpoelstra.com

INTRODUCING

Isaiah

I wonder if you've ever left a church service, women's conference, or Bible study determined to do better. Maybe your internal dialogue included intentions to pray regularly, show more kindness to others, or be a better person in general. This determination usually springs from a longing to grow spiritually and know God better. Yet where has all our white knuckle grasping at behavior modification gotten us? How's that "striving" been working out for you?

I can tell you how it has worked for me. My attempts at heart transformation have left me with guilt and frustration, and they have caused me to go backward rather than forwards in intimacy with God. When I've succeeded in the short term, I've often become prideful. Then in moments of failure, I've experienced shame. God doesn't want either of these postures for us.

Desiring spiritual change in our lives isn't a bad thing, we just have to guard against relying on our own effort to bring it about. As we embark together on a study of the prophet Isaiah's biblical book, we will discover a simple but life-changing truth: *Following God isn't about striving; it's about trusting God more.* The prophet Isaiah served as God's mouthpiece to the people of God and the surrounding nations. His message reverberates through our lives today as we read Isaiah's call to rely on the Lord.

Using the genres of poetry, narrative, and prophecy, Isaiah teaches that followers of God can trust His:

- Character
- Calendar
- Comfort
- Commands
- Correction
- Coming Again

That all sounds so good! However, I know by now that there are times when I say with my mouth, "I trust God," but my stress, worry, and lack of peace don't evidence that kind of faith. Trust can be complicated, especially when people in our lives have broken it. Perhaps someone you counted on for protection and provision let you down. Maybe you invested your time and energy into a church and left feeling betrayed or neglected. It can be easy to transfer our trust issues from people onto our relationship with God.

Then there are other times when we thought we put our trust in God, but the expectations we set for Him didn't materialize. He may have been working behind the scenes, but we couldn't see how at the time. When He doesn't do what we want Him to do, we can inch our way toward self-sufficiency without even realizing it.

Isaiah was human just like us, and yet he radically trusted God and called anyone who would listen to do the same. His message highlights freedom from captivity and light breaking through darkness for those who would heed his words. Anyone in need of a little freedom and light in their thoughts, attitudes, or actions? Hanging out with Isaiah over the next six sessions will be like filling a trust prescription with amazing side effects of hope and peace in your life and mine! Unpacking Isaiah's words will reveal that we can trust God more than our own human effort or the counterfeits the world suggests.

Isaiah has been referred to as "a Bible in miniature."[1] The book's sixty-six chapters and the Bible's sixty-six books include all genres of biblical literature, such as historical narrative, poetry, and prophecy. Some have compared Isaiah's first thirty-nine chapters with the thirty-nine books of the Old Testament because of the emphasis on God's judgment toward sin, while the last twenty-seven chapters parallel the New Testament's focus on God's grace.[2]

Isaiah has also been referred to as the fifth Gospel because of the number of Messianic references found in the book. Isaiah's words are quoted in the New Testament more times than any other Old Testament book. For Day Five of each session of our study, we'll look at the session's theme through a Messianic lens focusing on Jesus in Isaiah. I know it can be tempting to skip days of personal study here and there, especially as you get to the end of a week, but I want to encourage you to press on because of the treasure you'll find in studying Christ during the last study of each week.

Isaiah wrote messages of both judgment and hope. Pastor H. B. Charles wrote, "Real faith is ambidextrous. It can take blessings in one hand and trouble in the other, lifting both in the worship of the God who is worthy of our stubborn trust, complete obedience, and unceasing praise."[3] Throughout our study of Isaiah, we'll learn to be ambidextrous. Hopefully by the time we turn the last page, we will be able to lift both hands in worship. We won't be striving harder, but instead trusting more deeply the Faithful One who is so worthy of our utter dependence. These are broad strokes of what awaits us in Isaiah, but I'm already excited to know that in one book of the Bible we'll glimpse so many important biblical themes.

OPTIONS FOR STUDY

Any time we begin a new Bible study, it's important to set realistic expectations for ourselves based on our current season of life. I know in some seasons we have extra time for more in-depth study, Scripture memory work, and additional reading. Other times— such as when our faith is new, our schedule is packed, or our children are small—we don't want to bite off more than we can chew and feel frustrated for not meeting our goals. As we study Isaiah together, I hope you'll choose a study method that is realistic for you but also challenges you to grow in your spiritual rhythms. Consider the following options and prayerfully decide what will be the right fit for your current season and situation:

1. **Basic Study.** The basic study includes five days of content that combine study of Scripture with personal reflection and application. This includes looking up Scripture, reflecting, engaging in interactive activities, and answering questions.

   At the end of each day, you'll find a daily wrap-up, including a reflection question, prayer, and memory verse challenge.

2. In-Depth Study. If you feel up to more study, here are a few ideas I recommend:

   a. WATCH the teaching videos that accompany each session after completing the personal Bible study reading each week. You have access to video teaching that provides additional content to help you better understand and apply what you just studied in the previous session. You'll find detailed information for how to access the teaching videos that accompany this study on the card inserted in the back of your Bible study book. You'll also find a Video Viewer Guide page at the end of each session, where you can follow along with the videos.

   b. DISCUSS your study and the teaching videos with a group. If you're doing this study with a group, you can use the questions and prompts provided on the Group Discussion Guide pages to help you review the previous five days of study and discuss the video teaching together.

   c. READ through the book of Isaiah. Because of the volume and organization of Isaiah's book, we will study it according to major themes rather than chapter by chapter. For those of you (like me!) who like to start with the first chapter and go in order, the "Read Through Isaiah" reading plan (found on p. 184) will be helpful.

   d. MEMORIZE the weekly Bible verses. It is helpful to recite these verses with a partner, so find a friend in your group who is also choosing an in-depth option.

   e. ADD to your study by using a study Bible or any of these free commentaries:
   www.studylight.org/commentaries/
   www.biblestudytools.com/commentaries/
   www.biblegateway.com/resources/commentaries/
   https://biblehub.com/commentaries/
   www.blueletterbible.org/study.cfm

3. Keeping It Simple. Depending on your circumstances, you may want to modify your goals. Perhaps it will be a win if you attend group meetings, complete three out of five days of your study (don't skip Day Five though!), or make some other modification to your plan. Our desire is not to check boxes but to trust God more fully. Pray for guidance, and set your goal accordingly.

Take time now to decide which study option feels right for you, and check it below.

    __ 1. Basic Study
    __ 2. In-Depth Study
    __ 3. Keeping It Simple: I will *do what I can, meditate on what I am learning and not put unreal and expectation*

Be sure to let someone in your group know which option you have chosen so that you have some accountability and encouragement.

A NOTE FOR GROUP LEADERS

If you're leading a Bible study group through Isaiah, then first I want to say thank you! I have no doubt God will use you to encourage the women in your group as you walk through His Word together. Here are a few resources to help as you facilitate your group:

a. **DISCUSSION QUESTIONS** found on the Group Discussion Guide pages at the end of each week of study

b. **TEACHING VIDEOS** to watch at each group session. You'll find detailed information for how to access the teaching videos that accompany this study on the card inserted in the back of your Bible study book. At your first group meeting, watch the Session One video, discuss the questions provided, and make sure all the women in your group have their Bible study book. When you gather for Session Two, you'll watch the Session Two teaching video and then discuss what you studied during the week.

c. **A LEADER VIDEO** from me to you, available for free at **lifeway.com/isaiah**

d. Also don't miss the **FREE CHURCH PROMOTIONAL RESOURCES** found at **lifeway.com/isaiah**—including a PowerPoint® template, promotional poster, invite card, and bulletin insert—to help you promote the study in your church or neighborhood.

A FINAL WORD

I can't wait to get started on this journey alongside you. I don't want us to keep striving and falling into a cycle of guilt when it comes to our faith. Instead, we can pursue God's heart and seek to trust Him more. Out of that trust, I believe we will find comfort and peace to sustain us as we hold trouble in one hand and blessing in another. I'm praying that you will join me as we let go of striving and answer Isaiah's call to the trust the Lord!

Session One

VIDEO VIEWER GUIDE

To access the video teaching sessions, use the instructions in the back of your Bible study book.

Šā'an means _trust, to lean on, trust in + support_ .

> In that day the remnant left in Israel, the survivors in the house of Jacob, will no longer depend on allies who seek to destroy them. But they will faithfully trust the LORD, the Holy One of Israel.
> ISAIAH 10:20

Qāvâ means _the waiting, looking for, the hope, the_ .

> But those who trust in the LORD will find new strength. They will soar high on wings like eagles. They will run and not grow weary. They will walk and not faint.
> ISAIAH 40:31

Bāṭaḥ means _to be confident, to be bold + secure_
_____ .

> Trust in the LORD always,
> for the LORD GOD is the eternal Rock.
> ISAIAH 26:4

We don't always _drift_ in good directions.

Never changing _truth_ is what will help us navigate ever changing _times_ .

Isaiah has been referred to as the _5th_ Gospel.

In the first thirty-nine chapters of Isaiah it seems that God is _afflicting_ the comfortable, while in the last twenty-seven chapters God is _comforting_ the afflicted.

Session One
GROUP DISCUSSION GUIDE

LEADER: *Before your first meeting, watch the Leader Video posted at* **lifeway.com/isaiah**. *Use this guide to facilitate your group meeting. If your group members are watching the videos on their own, rather than together during your gathering, you'll want to select two or three questions from the days of personal study to add to your discussion time.*

SHARE: Guide each group member to share her name and the town where she was born.

WATCH the video "Session One: Introducing Isaiah" (23:25 minutes) together and follow along with the viewer guide on the previous page.

VIDEO DISCUSSION
1. *Discuss:* From the background information in this week's video, what is something new you learned about the book of Isaiah?
2. Turn in your Bibles to the following passages and ask volunteers to read them out loud: Isaiah 12:2; 25:9; 26:3-4; 40:31; 50:10. *Ask:* What stood out to you from these passages? *name of the lord = His character*

STUDY DISCUSSION
1. *Ask:* How does Isaiah's message of "striving less and trusting God more" resonate in your life today?
2. Turn to pages 7–8 and read aloud the section titled, "Options for Study." Give your group time to consider which level of study they will choose. Then ask each person to share which option she marked.
3. *Ask:* What is something you are looking forward to or hoping to learn as we begin studying the book of Isaiah?

REVIEW
Remind your group to complete the five days of personal study for Session Two: Trust God's Character. Take a moment to highlight the Big Idea for each day. These key points will be important to review at the end of their week of study.

PRAYER
Close your group meeting with a time of prayer.* Depending on the size of your group, consider breaking into smaller groups of two or three women and praying for each other. You might have a little extra time since this is the introductory week.

*Be sure to watch the leader video found at **lifeway.com/isaiah** for some ideas for varying your group's prayer time.

TRUST *God's* CHARACTER

SESSION TWO

We can't trust someone unless we know that person has our best interests in mind. When it comes to the Lord, you may know He loves you, but have you ever wondered why He isn't fixing something you really want to be fixed? This week, we'll explore God's character. Isaiah reveals the Lord as holy, as the One whom we should revere as Almighty. Isaiah also tells us that our God is forgiving and merciful—He transforms our crimson sins until they are white as snow.

I'm so glad you're joining me on this journey into deeper trust. As we take a fresh look at Isaiah's message in light of God's attributes, we'll understand that our Redeemer is passionately committed to us. We don't want our relationship with Him to be about temporary behavior modification; rather, we want to allow the Holy One of Israel to do real transforming work in our hearts. This won't be accomplished by swatting at our bad habits but by growing a bigger view of our God who longs for us to strive less and trust Him more.

MEMORY VERSE

"Come now, let's settle this,"
says the LORD.
"Though your sins are like scarlet,
I will make them as white as snow.
Though they are red like crimson,
I will make them as white
as wool."

ISAIAH 1:18

Without our forgiveness of sins, — gives of peace

Day One

PASSIONATE COMMITMENT

SCRIPTURE FOCUS
Isaiah 1

BIG IDEA
We can trust God because He is passionately committed to us.

I hurriedly pulled the clothes out of the dryer until I noticed a huge streak of blue on one of my favorite shirts. Upon closer inspection, I found that most of the articles in the load had similar marks. After rummaging around in the basket, I found a blue ink pen fully emptied of its contents. I had heard that hairspray could remove ink, so I repeatedly sprayed, rubbed, and rinsed until the Aqua Net® fumes were more than I could handle. Finally, I surrendered to the permanence of the stains and threw out the entire load. While the loss of those clothes frustrated me, I wasn't passionately committed to them. I tried to make them clean, but I couldn't.

At times in my life, I've felt like that stained laundry and wondered if I'm worth God's effort in the midst of all my struggles and failures. Can you relate? Thankfully, our God doesn't treat us as expendable. I hope today we can put those nagging thoughts behind us as we discover just how passionately committed the Lord is to His people.

Isaiah is a book of the Bible written more than twenty-seven hundred years ago by a man who obeyed God's call to be His prophet, God's mouthpiece to His people. Isaiah spoke to his original audience regarding current events, but also prophesied happenings that have since been fulfilled, like the birth of the Messiah, and some that have yet to come to fruition as they speak of the future return of Christ. As we move through this study, we'll attempt to practice good methods of interpretation to first look at Isaiah's intent for the initial recipients of his words but also the biblical principles that apply in our lives today. I hope you're as excited as I am to get started.

Isaiah's name means, "*Yahweh is salvation.*"[1]

SINS LIKE SCARLET

READ ISAIAH 1:1. Write down what you learn about Isaiah from the introduction to his book.

The Bible doesn't tell us anything about Isaiah's father Amoz, but some commentators suggest that Isaiah was connected to royalty because of his easy access to the kings mentioned here.[2] Others suggest that the Jewish tradition of Isaiah's royal birth is completely without merit.[3] While we want to get to know Isaiah, we'll need to be patient as his first vision tells us more about his people, the Judeans, than it tells us about his person.

> **NOW READ ISAIAH 1:2-5.** Record at least three things you learn about the character of God's people at the time of Isaiah's writing.
>
> •
>
> •
>
> •

Perhaps you listed rebelling against God, not recognizing God's care for them, or inviting judgment. Or you may have written descriptive words, such as *guilty, evil, sinful,* or *corrupt* (depending on your translation). Did you notice how Isaiah summoned the heavens and earth to listen to God's rebuke (v. 2)? And he used a comparison to donkeys and oxen to illustrate the nation's ingratitude toward God compared with how these animals trust and obey their masters (v. 3).

> **READ ISAIAH 1:6-9.** Summarize in a sentence the circumstances the people of God faced at the time of Isaiah's vision.

Sin brought suffering into the lives of God's people. Let's be clear: Not all of our problems are rooted in *personal* sin, but we would not have any problems if sin didn't exist. We live in a fallen world where even the most innocent children aren't immune to unspeakable suffering. We must exercise caution in assigning specific cause and effect to our trials, but oftentimes we can draw a connection between sin and suffering. Perhaps an infidelity brought consequences into your family, or a lie broke trust in a relationship. God's people reaped what they had sown, and the Lord didn't leave them guessing about what had Him so upset.

> **READ ISAIAH 1:10-15.** List some of the verbs God used in describing His reaction to their behavior.

Did you note some words and phrases like *hate, sick, stop, want no more*, or *cannot stand*? When God reacts this strongly to His beloved people, we should perk up and pay attention so that we can know what hurts His heart. These were some of the complaints He lodged against Isaiah's people: ceremonial display of sacrifices devoid of repentance and obedience; meaningless gifts and offerings; celebrations, fasting, and pious meetings for outward show; and praying to God while simultaneously preying on the innocent.

How would you sum up this behavior in one or two words?

Isaiah 1:4-17 uses the literary genre of an extended poem consisting of four elements: "a general indictment (v. 4), a lament about Israel's true and pitiful situation (vv. 5-9), a refusal to heed Israel in time of need (vv. 10-15), and a summons to reformation (vv. 16-17)."[4]

The word *hypocrisy* came to mind as I read these verses. It wasn't the *use* but the *abuse* of spiritual practices that brought such a strong reaction from God. The people were going through the motions of spiritual worship without a personal connection to the Lord and His laws. God called out the contradiction in their lives of uniting spiritual practices with unrepentant sin. In God's words, they lifted their hands in prayer, but those same hands were "covered with blood" (Isa. 1:15, CSB). God invites His people into relationship, and He expects repentance and obedience to follow.

Before we're too quick to condemn the rebellious people in these pages, let's take a moment to bring Isaiah's words a little closer to home. I know I can relate to projecting a spiritual image on the outside (social media, church services, group gatherings) while struggling to live the truths I espouse or failing to nurture my relationship with God—especially when no one is looking.

Reflect on any spiritual incongruity in your life recently. How have the truths we've read so far in Isaiah brought conviction? Think specifically about your thought life, judgments, attitudes, and actions.

Don't worry, we don't have to leave our first day of study on this heavy, somber note! We're just getting to the best part.

WHITE AS SNOW

READ ISAIAH 1:16-18. What hope do you see for the nation of Judah? What were some changes God required to restore their relationship to Him?

If God had hope for the stubborn, rebellious people of Judah, we know there is hope for us as well! No matter how far we've sunk in our depravity and sin, God remains committed to us, and He invites us to turn from our sin and turn toward Him. Only with repentant hearts are we able to live as the people God created us to be—those who love Him and love others.

The "scarlet" or "crimson" mentioned in Isaiah 1:18 referenced a dye made from an insect that permanently marked garments, such as the clothing of the high priest and the hangings in the tabernacle.[5] The hearers would have understood it to be something like the ink stains in my laundry with no way to remove the color once it had been applied. As Christ followers today, we see in this verse a picture of the work of Jesus on our behalf. Through the blood of Christ—not through any amount of human scrubbing—the stain of our sin can be removed permanently.

LOVED AND FORGIVEN

Throughout the pages of Isaiah, we'll find God encouraging His people that forgiveness is available. His plan to send Jesus was already in motion—the people of Isaiah's day could believe faithfully that a Messiah would come. In the same way, we can rely on the truth that Jesus makes our scarlet sins "as white as snow" (v. 18).

You can trust God's character because He is passionately committed to His people. His plan is for your cleansing and renewal. The Lord hates sin because of its destructive power, but He loves and is committed to redeeming sinners!

The assurance of forgiveness for those who repent is continually confirmed throughout the book of Isaiah (12:1; 30:18-19; 33:24; 38:17; 40:1-2; 43:25; 44:22; 59:20) pointing ultimately to Christ's sacrifice—prophesied as the Suffering Servant in Isaiah 52:13–53:12.[6]

And one more thing: You can't out-sin God's grace. Let's settle this right at the beginning of our study. Lies the enemy may be using against you like . . .

- You are just too much to handle;
- You will never be able to change;
- Your sins are worse than other people's sins; or
- The stain of your mistakes will always follow you.

. . . are NOT true. Your God is *passionately committed* to you!

Take a moment to feel the full weight of God's passion and forgiveness for you. Write your name in the blank:

"Come now, let's settle this," says the LORD.
"Though [Hanya's (yours) 's] sins are like scarlet,
I will make them as white as snow.
Though they are red like crimson,
I will make them as white as wool."
ISAIAH 1:18

I need constant reminders of these truths about God's love, His wrath toward sin, and the sacrifice of His own Son to remove my sin stains. Even if it feels like your life has been through the spin cycle followed by heat that set the stains of your past, you can become white as snow because the God you serve is passionately committed to you.

DAILY WRAP-UP

Today we focused on this truth: *We can trust God because He is passionately committed to us.* How would you summarize your personal takeaway from today's study?

PRAYER

Lord, thank You for Your passion and commitment to me. Most days I don't feel white like snow. I battle against the problems in life and my own sin on a regular basis. Help me to strive less and trust more. I'm so glad You don't require me to earn my way to You through religious works and instead invite me into a personal relationship. Remind me of this truth often because I'm so prone to forget it! In Jesus's name, amen.

MEMORY VERSE ACTIVITY

Read Isaiah 1:18 aloud three times. You can find it printed on this page.

Day Two

HOLY AND HIGHER

During my children's elementary school years, they had chore charts
to give them structure and responsibility. However, when they didn't
accomplish all their tasks, we would have a conversation about allowance
reduction or possible consequences. Can you imagine if one of my
children said, "I know I've been slacking off recently. If I get all my
chores done every day this week and even do some of my sibling's chores,
can I remain your child?" They understood that they were assigned work
because they were part of our family, not that they were working to stay
in it. Sometimes I can bring a "working to earn my place in the family"
mentality into my relationship with the Lord.

As we dig into Isaiah 6 today, we find a progression of belief, which leads
to a sense of belonging, which then results in transformed behavior.
The order of this progression is important:

SEEING THE LORD (6:1-4)   →   BELIEF

SEEING OURSELVES (6:5-7)   →   BELONGING BECAUSE
GOD CLEANSES OUR SIN

SEEING OUR NEXT STEPS (6:8) → BEHAVIOR

I often desire clarity in decisions but first need to focus on the Lord—
and myself in relation to Him—so that I can have a proper perspective
to receive direction. Let's begin by seeing the Lord's character through
Isaiah's vision.

SEEING THE LORD

> **READ ISAIAH 6:1-4.** Either sketch or write a short
> description of the scene Isaiah encountered.

The Lord speaks to the people in anger or disappointment. They have not
looked to the Lord as the Holy one. Their relationship is no more matured
or understood than the animals. The nation was sinful, corrupt r
abandoned by the Lord. turned away from him. There is nothing good
in them

SCRIPTURE
FOCUS
Isaiah 6

BIG IDEA
We can trust
God because
He is holy.

One distinction of Isaiah's writing is his use of the name for God as the "Holy One of Israel." While it is found thirty-one times in the Old Testament, no fewer than twenty-five are found in Isaiah.[8]

When words are repeated twice in Scripture, it indicates superiority (like "Lord of lords" in Ps. 136:3). Repeating a word three times indicates that this is the ultimate/highest point of that feature. Isaiah used "holy, holy, holy" to mean God is absolutely, perfectly holy. He is more holy than everyone and everything else.

Whether you drew or wrote the details, take a moment to visualize this scene. The ultimate authority of heaven and earth sits on His throne wearing a robe that fills the temple. He is attended by angels called seraphim who call out to each other, "Holy, holy, holy" (v. 3). This is the only biblical passage where heavenly beings are called "seraphim." "The seraphs are bright creatures, for the word means 'burning ones'; yet they hide their faces from the greater brightness and glory of the Lord."[7] Their words shake the room and smoke fills the entire temple.

If you were Isaiah and actually witnessed this with your own eyes, what reactions might you have had?

Total horror — astonished that the people did not honor the Lord. The corruption and evil ways — removing God from their lives would amount in total loss of faith in God. "There is nothing saved in them" and God does not listen because He is seperate + apart

I think I would have been overcome with the holiness or "otherness" of it all. No movie, novel, or dream could compare with a glimpse of the living God. While God forgives and loves us as sinners, desiring a relationship with us like we saw yesterday, we should not be tempted to bring Him down to our human level. These verses remind us that He is holy. The Hebrew for holy is *qadowsh,* which means "sacred, holy, Holy One, saint, set apart."[9] To say God is holy means He is set apart. He is not like us. He is perfect in all He does. He rules supremely and receives the worship of an array of heavenly beings.

Write a few sentences below praising God as the Holy One you worship today.

Once we see the Lord, we can then gain clarity about our own position in relation to Him.

READ ISAIAH 6:5-7. Summarize Isaiah's response and the angel's actions in your own words.

ISAIAH'S RESPONSE	ANGEL'S ACTION
I am ruined - a man of Unclean lips	for I have seen the "KING the LORD OF HOSTS
He touched my mouth with it + said	Seraphim flps with a burning coal + touched my mouth · Taken from the alter
	Behold, this has touched your lips and your iniqity and ~~this~~ is taken away and your sin is forgiven

In response to God's holiness, Isaiah recognized his own sinfulness. He didn't try to hide or pretend; instead, he confessed his predicament. Let's take a moment to join him today.

Write a brief response to the Lord of how you feel about your own sinfulness in light of His holiness.

My sinfulness is so great - not only in my heart (which I know and feel) But to others around me. I have such a hard time relinquishing my sins even though they are forgiven. I must trust Him in the light of His Holiness. I feel guilt instead of freedom and KNOW ABSOLUTELY I am forgiven and remember J.C. died for my sins, removed the guilt, forgave me and gave me the freedom to always believe in the power of God

Confession as a spiritual practice should lead us toward God rather than away from Him. I love that the Lord didn't shame Isaiah in his brokenness, but instead God removed his guilt. The imagery of the burning coal taken from the altar reminds us that the Lord longs to cleanse us as well. Jesus offered His life as payment for our sins. His altar was a cross where He removed our guilt and forgave our sins through His shed blood.

Every Gospel references the words from Isaiah 6:9-10 in connection with the parable of the sower (Matt. 13:14-15; Mark 4:10-12; Luke 8:10; John 12:39-41), and the last verse in chapter 6 speaks of Israel's stump becoming a holy seed.

READ ISAIAH 6:8-13. What did the Lord ask, and how did Isaiah respond (v. 8)?

Whom shall I send and who will go for us? "Here am I, send me!

What is your initial reaction to the message the Lord gave Isaiah (vv. 9-13)?

He can hear the Lord.

First, Isaiah saw the Lord (Isa. 6:1-4); then, he saw himself clearly (Isa. 6:5-7). Only then did he receive the call to prophesy (Isa. 6:8). The message the Lord gave him to share wasn't the touchy-feely inspiration I was expecting. The Lord knew that His own people would reject Him for many generations and reap the consequences of their choices. Verses like these give us an opportunity to trust that God knows and sees more than we do.

As Isaiah's calling reveals, God's instructions aren't always what we're expecting. In Isaiah's eagerness to answer God's call, it's hard to believe he knew the difficult task that awaited him and the challenging words God would have him deliver. The moments when life doesn't go as we think it should provide the clearest opportunities to exercise trust in our relationship with Him. Oftentimes the only next step we can take is one of acknowledging to God, "Here I am."

Reflect on a time when what was happening in your life didn't match up with what you thought the Lord should be doing. What were some of the questions you asked God at that time?

Why am I being so hurt by John? When will it ever end.

When my daughter was twelve years old and lost all her hair to an autoimmune disease called alopecia, she begged God for hair. She prayed until she began to doubt His goodness and power because nothing happened. Perhaps you've encountered something much more significant than hair loss, and when the Lord didn't intervene, you began to lose trust in Him. These are the moments when we need reminders of His character so that we can press into our faith.

READ ISAIAH 55:8-9 and underline the words <u>thoughts</u> and <u>ways</u>:

"My thoughts are nothing like your thoughts," says the LORD.
"And my ways are far beyond anything you could imagine.
For just as the heavens are higher than the earth,
so my ways are higher than your ways
and my thoughts higher than your thoughts."

I wonder if you can look back and see something in your past from the perspective that God's thoughts and ways were higher than yours. Write down anything that comes to mind.

The difficulty will Jill when Mom + Dad died

You may not always understand what God is doing in the moment, but you can always trust Him! The God of Isaiah is the same God who invites you to be close to Him. He knows you don't always follow all His instructions, and thankfully, you don't have to earn your way into His family. If you have believed in Him by faith, then you belong to Him. He loves you and knows better than you do what is best for your life because His thoughts and ways are higher than yours.

DAILY WRAP-UP

Today we focused on this truth: *We can trust God because He is holy.* How would you summarize your personal takeaway from today's study?

I just have to trust God will heal my woes, circumstances and my behavior. I simply can not solve anything according to my will.

Lord, thank You for reminding me of Your holiness. Help me not to forget Your greatness and power, especially when it comes to trusting You with real life situations. When I drift into grappling for power over my circumstances, help me to remember that Your thoughts and ways are higher than mine so I can trust You! In Jesus's name, amen.

MEMORY VERSE ACTIVITY

Read Isaiah 1:18 aloud one time. Then write it down in your book or on a separate piece of paper.

Day Three

POWER IN THE NAME

**SCRIPTURE
FOCUS**

Isaiah 45

BIG IDEA

We can trust God
because He makes
Himself known.

Recently my husband and I provided respite care to two brothers who
were entering the foster care system. They didn't know us, and the air
was thick as we tried to welcome them without asking prying questions
about their situation. Over the next several weeks we got to know each
other as we shared meals, played board games, and talked on the long
drive back and forth to school. Both boys expressed surprise that we
didn't yell at them when they did something wrong. In time they saw that
we genuinely wanted what was best for them. By the time a placement
was found much closer to their city, our goodbyes were teary because we
had come to love and trust each other in a short time walking with them
through difficult circumstances. Trust grows over time as we get to know
someone is safe and has our best interests at heart.

> **Who is someone you've grown to trust as you've
> gotten to know him or her well? What makes you
> trust that person?**

Michael Fleis - He listens - never judges
gently talks to me - we can talk honestly to
each other and I know he will not spread anything
we talk about as gossip
Otherwise - I really don't trust anyone because
there is too much disappointment

We'll continue to hear Isaiah mount a call to trust the Lord throughout the
pages of his book. One of the best ways for us to trust God and understand
His character is by examining some of His names revealed in His Word.
God said through Isaiah, "But I will reveal my name to my people, and
they will come to know its power. Then at last they will recognize that I am
the one who speaks to them" (Isa. 52:6). There is power in God's name!

Many different names and descriptions for God appear in Scripture
because His greatness can't be embodied in just one. But for the sake
of our study today, we're going to focus on the names of God found in
Isaiah 45. I've chosen this passage because it includes so many different
names for God that are used throughout the book of Isaiah, and we can
flip around our Bibles less by camping out here.

READ ISAIAH 45. Record God's names in the chart below. (Several are repeated throughout the chapter, so we'll record only the first mentions.) I've also included a space for you to record any thoughts, insights, or comments regarding each name. (I did the first two for you so you get the idea.)

VERSE	NAME/ DESCRIPTION OF GOD	OPTIONAL COMMENTS
1	LORD	LORD in all caps refers to Yahweh in the Bible.
3	God of Israel	He calls us by name.
9	Maker	his plans for the future. Created Heaven + earth
11	Holy One of Israel	the LORD will reveal the future because he is the Holy One
13	Lord of hosts	keeps his promises ?
14	God is wt you	there is only one God to be worshiped no others
15	Savior	to be saved by the Lord to salvation

What stands out to you as you look over the chart you filled in?

I am so glad I am a believer of God who has promised me salvation. I have been saved

You may have been surprised by how many varied names you found, such as *God, Creator, LORD of Hosts, Holy One of Israel, Savior,* and so on. These different expressions are just the tip of the iceberg when it comes to the book of Isaiah. Eighteen times throughout his book, Isaiah referred to God as the "Sovereign LORD" (NLT)—and "Lord GOD" in the CSB)

—which is *Adonai Yahweh* in Hebrew. *Redeemer* is used in thirteen instances with other mentions like *Immanuel, the First and the Last,* our *Judge, Shepherd, Warrior, Rock, Mighty One,* and *Everlasting God* also expanding our knowledge of God's character.

Let's take a moment to focus on just four names we discovered in Isaiah 45 and see how they can help us know and trust God more. We'll explore *Yahweh, Elohim, Creator,* and *Savior,* and then you'll have the opportunity to write a trust statement related to each name.

YAHWEH

Yahweh is translated using capital letters—LORD—to distinguish it from *Adonai* which most Bibles render "Lord" in lowercase. *Yahweh* is the personal name God used when talking to Moses at the burning bush, and God described it as "my eternal name, my name to remember for all generations" (Ex. 3:15). Most scholars associate YHWH with the verb "to be," so this name is sometimes defined as "the self-existent One."[10] Yahweh has always been and continues to be completely self-sustaining and self-sufficient.

> **Take a moment now to fill in the blanks as you think about Yahweh and the concerns or blessings in your life:**
>
> I can trust Yahweh with _____
> because He is _____.

ELOHIM

When you recorded *God* on your chart, the original Hebrew was either *El* or *Elohim.* (It varied in Isaiah 45. *Elohim* is actually a plural form of *El.*) *Elohim* is used more than two thousand times in the Old Testament, making it the word used to identify God most often in Scripture.[12] While the original audience wouldn't have understood the plural name as referring to the Trinity, we know that God is Father, Son, and Holy Spirit because He has progressively revealed Himself over time.

Scripture tells us that our God is transcendent, creative, and powerful. At times I try to reduce God to something I can understand and define, but we can't put Elohim in a box. He exists outside of time. He made the beginning and already knows the end. This stretches my brain to its edges because I live by a calendar and a clock.

Fill in this blank: I can trust Elohim today because He is a God who

_____

_____.

CREATOR

Isaiah 45:9 referenced God as *Maker* or *Creator*. The Hebrew word is *Yatsar*, which means "to form, fashion, frame."[13] Isaiah used the illustration of the potter and his clay to help the people understand God's authority to shape us according to His design. Over the course of our study, we will also find three mentions of God as the Potter and His people as clay (29:16; 41:25; 64:8).

Isaiah's original audience argued against God's instructions, but Isaiah reminded them of God's position. When we see God as our Maker, we learn to trust Him even through painful processes of shaping, cutting away, and then firing to solidify us according His design. As we consider God as former, fashioner, and framer in our lives, we can loosen our grip on our illusion of control and concentrate on being clay that is moldable in His hands.

Fill in this blank: Creator God, soften and mold me when it comes to

_____

_____.

SAVIOR

While God is *Yahweh* (self-existent), *Elohim* (our God), *Creator* (with complete authority to mold and shape us), may we never lose sight that He is also *Savior*, the One who longs to save us. In Isaiah 45, both verses 15 and 21 used *Savior* to describe our God. Jesus reminded us of God's desire to save us. Just after He declared that God loved the world and gave His Son so that those who believe in Him "will not perish but have eternal life" (John 3:16), Jesus said this: "God sent his Son into the world not to judge the world, but to save the world through him" (John 3:17).

Both Isaiah's name in Hebrew and Jesus's name in Greek mean "Yahweh is salvation." We never want to forget God's power and authority, but we also don't want to lose sight of His goodness to deliver us from sin.

MEMORY VERSE ACTIVITY

Write down Isaiah 1:18. Also record one thought you have as you read over this verse.

Fill in these blanks for our final name today:

I can trust God to rescue me from _____

_____

because His name means _____.

We just scratched the surface with four names found in Isaiah today. Which one of the names we focused on most resonated with your current thoughts and circumstances? Why?

I'm so thankful that we serve a God who invites us to draw near (Jas. 4:8). Just as it takes time to develop trust in human relationships, our trust in the Lord grows as we pursue a deeper walk with Him.

DAILY WRAP-UP

Today we focused on this truth: *We can trust God because He makes Himself known.* How would you summarize your personal takeaway from today's study?

Day Four

THE PATHWAY TO PEACE

I woke up frustrated and discouraged after a battle with worry in the middle of the night. Don't laugh when I tell you what I was obsessing over because it seems so ridiculous in hindsight. My highly allergic daughters had just convinced my husband and me to allow them to buy pet birds since cats and dogs made them sick. I laid awake fretting about the smell in our house, the annoying sounds the birds made, and then imagined ways to get rid of them without breaking my daughters' hearts.

Looking back, I can't believe how over-focused I became on something that wasn't that important in the grand scheme of life. This worry, fear, and fixating on small problems that I blow out of proportion has been a perennial problem for me. Whether our fears are overblown or completely appropriate because life has thrown us some curveballs, most of us struggle to find peace in the midst of our problems. Isaiah's message gives us hope that we can make internal choices that lead to peace when we face external forces that tempt us to worry.

SCRIPTURE FOCUS
Isaiah 7:1-9; 8

BIG IDEA
We can trust God because in Him is perfect peace.

EXTERNAL FORCES

READ ISAIAH 7:1-2. Describe how the king of Judah and his people responded to the external forces coming against them.

King Ahaz faced threats from two countries. One of these was Judah's own family. Israel was the Northern Kingdom made of ten tribes that separated from Judah after Solomon's reign. As we saw at the start of Isaiah 7, Israel teamed up with the pagan nation of Syria to come against Judah. Sometimes when our pain comes from unexpected places—like family, friends, or a church or job we thought was safe—our fears can feel magnified.

What would you identify as a current challenge coming from external forces? What stressors are threatening your peace right now?

Thankfully now that my twins are in college, I'm no longer stressing over their pets' noises and smells. However, I find that the problems my adult children face often keep me up at night. Moving from authority to advisor hasn't been an effortless transition for me. We all have challenges from external forces whether they're happening directly to us or impacting us through the people we love. Maybe your situation has nothing to do with children, but perhaps a medical diagnosis, financial crisis, or relational conflict has left you feeling like the people of Judah—"shaking in a storm" (v. 2). So, what do we do when we feel the impact of outside forces tossing us about in life? Let's keep reading in Isaiah 7 for some practical wisdom that will help in those moments.

READ ISAIAH 7:3-9. What did Isaiah tell the king to stop doing in verse 4?

According to verse 9, what needed to happen in order for the Lord to make him stand firm?

The Lord told Ahaz to stop worrying. "Do not fear" is a command issued often throughout Scripture. Philippians 4:6 tells us "don't worry about anything." That sounds so good, but how do we do that? Like when we can't sleep, can't stop recycling our thoughts and emotions, and feel like peace is a luxury we aren't afforded in *our* marriages, *our* jobs, *our* finances, *our* health situations, and so on? One commentator summarized God's instruction to stand firm in faith as "trust or bust!"[14]

As you reflect on the challenge you identified above, what are the alternatives to trusting God?

When I choose not to trust, I often revert to worry, excessive planning, or complaining about the problem to others. I could definitely put all those in the "bust" category! The Lord doesn't leave us without help in these moments. He wants to help us stand firm in our faith as He instructed Ahaz to do when facing his fears.

READ ISAIAH 8. Record in the chart below what you learn about God's offer to care for His people and His instructions to help them grow in trust. (I did the first ones for you. Answers will vary by translation.)

GOD'S CARE FOR HIS PEOPLE	GOD'S INSTRUCTIONS
Verse 6: Provided gently flowing waters	Verse 11: Don't think like everyone else (NLT). Don't follow the way of this people (NIV). Don't walk in the way of this people (ESV).
Verse 10:	Verse 12:
Verse 14:	Verse 13:
	Verse 16:
	Verse 17:
	Verse 19:
	Verse 20:

God longed to care for His people like gently flowing waters. He was with them and was a place of safety for them. He alone could be their pathway to peace, yet so many times they rejected Him. They didn't trust Him to care for them and instead looked to human strength, false gods, and mediums for guidance.

INTERNAL CHOICES

MEMORY VERSE ACTIVITY

Attempt to write out Isaiah 1:18 from memory, then check to see how you did.

READ ISAIAH 26:3. What are some practical ways to fix your thoughts on the Lord when you find yourself shaken by external forces?

Here are a few ideas I've implemented when I find myself struggling to embrace God's peace in the midst of a storm: Write a list of God's attributes or names in my journal. Go for a walk or change my physical posture to redirect my body and mind. Call or text a friend and ask her to pray for my mental focus to shift.

Ahaz had decisions to make and so do we. We may not have a prophet who can tell us exactly what the future holds, but we can think differently than others with reasoned responses rather than knee-jerk reactions. We can decide to stop striving and trust God. When we do, we'll find the power to obey commands like "stop worrying," "don't fear," and "have faith," even when life is scary. We can find perfect peace when we fix our thoughts on Him. I hope that no matter what type of challenge you are facing today, you can find peace in knowing that God loves you and longs to be your Defender!

DAILY WRAP-UP

Today we focused on this truth: *We can trust God because in Him is perfect peace.* How would you summarize your personal takeaway from today's study?

Day Five

IMMANUEL, GOD WITH US

After spending large amounts of time with people—even people I dearly love—I need a break. I want to shut myself in my room with a "keep out" sign on the door. Being an introvert was challenging when my four kids were small, but as they have all left the nest, I've experienced the flip side of time alone. When my husband works long hours and the kids are all busy with their own schedules, occasionally feelings of loneliness emerge. I guess too much of a good thing is true even for introverts! Following God doesn't immunize us against feelings of loneliness, either. They can even creep into our relationship with the Lord.

When God seems a million miles away or when our prayers feel like they are hitting the ceiling, we can encounter spiritual loneliness. During these seasons, we might entertain questions like:

- *Is the Lord still with me?*

- *How can I trust that He is still here even when I've messed up again, disappointed people I love, or questioned my beliefs?*

- *What should I do in moments when I can't sense God's nearness?*

If someone came to you with these types of questions, how would you advise them? Write a sentence or two that you might say in response.

Just try to pray and ask God with strength to give you an answer. He will hear you and when the time is right according to his will you will get the response. Trust in God—He is always with you

As we read Isaiah's words today, we will draw out facts that will help us trust God when our feelings aren't on board. Even when we don't sense God at work, He is. He is Immanuel, God with us. We just need to rediscover what we already have: a God who went to great lengths to redeem His relationship with His people.

SCRIPTURE
FOCUS
Isaiah 7:10-25; 9:1-7

BIG IDEA

We can trust
God because
He is with us.

A SIGN OF HOPE

READ ISAIAH 7:10-25. Draw a line from the person to the action.

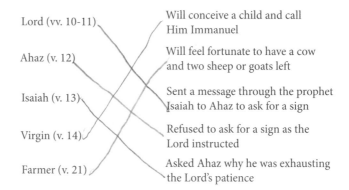

Lord (vv. 10-11)

Ahaz (v. 12)

Isaiah (v. 13)

Virgin (v. 14)

Farmer (v. 21)

Will conceive a child and call Him Immanuel

Will feel fortunate to have a cow and two sheep or goats left

Sent a message through the prophet Isaiah to Ahaz to ask for a sign

Refused to ask for a sign as the Lord instructed

Asked Ahaz why he was exhausting the Lord's patience

What stuck out to you in these verses?

not right   You need to ask for a sign – don't refuse because the Lord can make things happen that could be against for not asking so be grateful for what the Lord gives you during bad times

> At the time Isaiah was written, curds (or butter or cream) and honey were good foods even considered self-indulgent in their culture.[15]

God invited Ahaz to reach out in faith, but Ahaz hid behind rules he didn't even follow to deny the Lord. Testing God was forbidden in the law (Deut. 6:16), but Ahaz twisted the command rather than heed God's invitation. It isn't testing God to do as He says! This exasperated Isaiah. Even though Ahaz didn't specify a sign, the Lord gave him one anyway.

This prophecy regarding a virgin has sparked much theological debate. I always thought this verse was just about Jesus the Messiah, but it also had significance in Isaiah's day. It was fulfilled for the original readers of Isaiah's message because we know that only a year or two after the prophecy was given the nations of Syria and Israel (the ones who threatened Judah) were destroyed by Assyria (Isa. 7:16). Although we don't know the identity of the mother or the child, the time frame of Isaiah's sign fit with historical events.

> The apostle Paul described people like Ahaz when he wrote, "They will act religious, but they will reject the power that could make them godly. Stay away from people like that!" (2 Tim. 3:5)

We also know that this sign had future implications. One commentator described his opinion this way, "I believe that the sign as originally given had a single meaning but a double significance. Its meaning is that God is with us and we need not fear what other human beings may do to us."[16]

While the verse has only one meaning, it had a double fulfillment that would come seven hundred years apart. First, it was significant to Ahaz as a challenge not to seek alliances with foreign nations like Assyria for help since God was with him.

Second, the Gospel of Matthew helps us see its fulfillment in the birth of Jesus. In Matthew 1, we learn that an angel appeared to Joseph giving greater insight into Isaiah's words:

> "And she will have a son, and you are to name him
> Jesus, for he will save his people from their sins."
> All of this occurred to fulfill the Lord's
> message through his prophet:
> "Look! The virgin will conceive a child!
> She will give birth to a son,
> and they will call him Immanuel,
> which means 'God is with us.'"
> MATTHEW 1:21-23

Signs like the one given in Isaiah 7:14 confirm God's long-term plan and commitment to His people. One scholar described the fullness of meaning in Matthew's words as "inspired reapplications of the inspired words."[17] The meaning is clear for Isaiah's day, Matthew's day, and ours: God is with us.

Take a moment to consider what the Messiah's name—Immanuel— means for you. What responses come to the surface as you consider that God is with you today in whatever circumstances you're facing?

God is with us
WONDERFUL
HOPEFULL
GRATEFUL

No matter what's going on in our lives, we can trust that Immanuel is with us. This takes active faith because our human defaults lead us toward distraction, self-pity, and lies when we feel alone. Isaiah's prophetic words remind us to lean into the truth of Immanuel with intentionality, and his message about this future child didn't end in chapter 7. Knowing that someone is with us is one thing, but when we discover that the person alongside us is "Wonderful," "Mighty," "Everlasting," and a "Prince," well that adds a whole new layer to what it means to have God with us.

Isaiah 9:1-7 uses past tense verbs in the Hebrew because Isaiah's hope was so certain, he wrote as though it had already happened.[18]

READ ISAIAH 9:1-7. What was the name of the region that would be filled with glory in the future?

Zebulun + Naphtali

What would the people see (vv. 1-2)?

The great light

What would be broken (v. 4)?

National Israel, away from bondage

What names were given for the child (v. 6)?

Wonderful counselor, Mighty God, Eternal Father, Prince of Peace

What would His government be like? What would make this happen (v. 7)?

one of justice + righteousness. The zeal of the LORD of hosts will accomplish this

Let's look closer at the names for the Promised One found in verse 6 and what they reveal to us about His character:

- **Wonderful Counselor** literally means "wonder-planner" or "wonder-working planner."[19]

- **Mighty God** emphasizes power like that of a champion in battle.

 - **Everlasting Father** may seem an odd title for the Son of God, but it highlights the Messiah's timeless concern, care, and discipline of His people.[20]

- **Prince of Peace** suggests an army commander, but unlike most princes, this commander's ultimate goal is peace.

Put a star next to the name you needed to hear today. Why did you choose that name?

How did the passages we read today land in your soul? Record any thoughts, questions, or insights you gained from Isaiah 9:1-7.

God has a plan - going from darkness to light the nation will be glad in his presence

I don't know what you're walking through right now, but I'm sure there have been times when you could relate to living in a land that feels dark (Isa. 9:2). The news is full of stories of tragedy, injustice, and difficulty. The darkness isn't only "out there" in the world. We often personally trudge through grief, complicated relationships, health problems, job losses, or other trials that can leave us in a dark place. When we focus our eyes on Jesus, we make our fundamental reality one that's focused on hope.

Can you see why Isaiah is referred to as the fifth Gospel? God is always with us, and His plans are much bigger than we can imagine. At the heart of Isaiah's message is the hope of the gospel: God sent His only Son, Jesus, to earth, and He offered the perfect sacrifice—Jesus's very life—to cleanse us from our sins: And because Jesus went into death with us, He can bring us out with Him.[21] We end our week of study with great hope knowing that God is not only with us in this life, but because He is Immanuel, we can be with Him in the next! Darkness and despair don't get the final say in our lives.

DAILY WRAP-UP

Today we focused on this truth: *We can trust God because He is with us.* **How would you summarize your personal takeaway from today's study?**

Session Two
VIDEO VIEWER GUIDE

To access the video teaching sessions, use the instructions in the back of your Bible study book.

We have to let God be _____ if we're going to be _____ to Him.

We want to get some _____ about God's _____ to remind ourselves why we can trust Him.

God is the _____ and _____ (Isa. 29:16; 45:9; 64:8).

We can trust God and trust His character because He is _____ and _____ (Isa. 6:1-8; 55:9).

Once we get some clarity about His _____, then we'll get some clarity about our _____.

God _____ the rebellious (Isa. 1:18).

WOW: _____

_____

WOE: _____

_____

ACTION STEP: Fix your thoughts on God. Pick one of these things to focus on:

1. List the attributes of God using the ABCs method.

2. Remind yourself of the names of God from Day Three of your study.

3. Learn your memory verse for this week—Isaiah 1:18—and focus on that truth.

Session Two

GROUP DISCUSSION GUIDE

SHARE: What is something you have created? (Think: art, recipe, an organization plan)

WATCH the video "Session Two: Trust God's Character" (25:21 minutes) together and follow along with the viewer guide on the previous page.

MEMORY VERSE

Review Isaiah 1:18 and give the group an opportunity to recite it aloud.

VIDEO DISCUSSION

1. *Ask:* Which character quality of God resonated with you from the video teaching?
2. *Discuss:* How does knowing God's character help you to trust Him more in your everyday life? Share practical examples.

STUDY DISCUSSION

1. Call on a volunteer to read aloud Isaiah 1:16-20. Ask women to share how they answered the Day One Daily Wrap-Up question (p. 18): *How would you summarize your personal takeaway from today's study?*
2. Discuss some of the attributes of God that stood out to you from the throne-room scene in Isaiah 6, which you studied in Day Two.
3. Remind your group of the four names for God we studied in Day Three: *Yahweh, Elohim, Creator,* and *Savior.* Guide women to share how they filled in the blank to this statement found on page 28: *I can trust God to rescue me from* _____ *because His name means* _____.
4. Call on someone to read Isaiah 26:3 out loud. Discuss practical ways to fix your thoughts on God in everyday life.
5. Read Isaiah 9:6-7. Ask for responses to the Day Five Daily Wrap-Up question (p. 37), *How would you summarize your personal takeaway from today's study?*

REVIEW

Review the Big Idea for each of the five days of study. Ask for final thoughts or questions regarding the study of God's character from Isaiah this week.

PRAYER REQUESTS

Lead women to write prayer requests on a provided note card, and pass the card to the woman on the right so each woman is being prayed for during the week.

TRUST *God's* CALENDAR

SESSION THREE

Trusting God's timing sounds good on paper, but it isn't so easy when God's calendar and ours don't seem to line up. Our culture has done everything possible to eliminate waiting. We can stream a movie, order take-out food, or buy something with a few simple clicks and get it that same day! Waiting on God can be challenging when it may seem like He doesn't respond as fast as Amazon®. Yet Isaiah reminds us that God is never early, and He is never late. He is always right on time. When we get impatient and strive more, we often find ourselves trusting less. This week we'll learn from King Hezekiah some lessons about trusting God's calendar in our own lives. Sometimes Hezekiah got it right, and other times he took a short-sighted view. As we explore Isaiah's message together, we'll learn to surrender our timelines in order to trust that our Creator knows the best timing for our moves, events, educations, reconciliations, health, and every other agenda we are pushing in our lives and the lives of those we love.

MEMORY VERSE

So the LORD must wait for you to come to him so he can show you his love and compassion. For the LORD is a faithful God. Blessed are those who wait for his help.

ISAIAH 30:18

Day One

WAITING AND PRAYING

BIG IDEA

In the waiting period between our trouble and God's rescue, we pray.

My daughter told me she was tired of people telling her to trust God. She had begged Him to make her hair grow back after her alopecia diagnosis. Despite years of prayers, though, she remained completely bald with no eyelashes or eyebrows. She knew all the Sunday School answers about God's love and power. But her real-life circumstances caused her to question why a God who loved her and had the power to heal her didn't do so. She wondered if the Lord was unable or unwilling.

Have you ever gone through a long period of waiting that challenged your trust in the Lord? If so, describe that season or situation in a few sentences.

I have waited for years for God to relieve me from my mental illness. This disease has affected me negatively my whole life.

This week our focus in Isaiah will center around trusting God's calendar, which means surrendering to His timing over ours. When God doesn't act as quickly as we'd like, we can revert to striving in our human strength to gain our desired result rather than seeking postures that position us for trust. For me that often looks like freaking out (worry, fear) or excessive planning.

What would you add to this list of reactions you have when God doesn't seem to be working on your timetable?

I simply keep thinking that I have complete control to fix our troubles. Will we be able to live on S.S. for the rest of our lives. I want to know if things will happen with all of the gov't policies that are scary. Will we be able to afford to be safe?

King Hezekiah's story shows us one example of what it looks like to trust God's plan even when we face circumstances that threaten our security. Before we start reading, let's review the biblical timeline that leads up to Hezekiah:

930 BC	729/8 BC	722 BC	715 BC	701 BC
The twelve tribes of Israel split into the Northern Kingdom of Israel and the Southern Kingdom of Judah.[1]	King Ahaz's son Hezekiah began to reign in Judah (likely alongside his father as co-regent).[2]	Assyria conquered and exiled the Northern Kingdom of Israel (2 Kings 18:11-12).[3]	King Ahaz died and Hezekiah reigned solo in Judah.[4]	Hezekiah gave the Assyrians all of Judah's silver and gold to keep them from invading but they still sent an army to threaten attack if they would not agree to exile (2 Kings 18:14-16).[5]

In spite of Hezekiah's payoff, the commander of the Assyrian army came to threaten Judah during the days of Isaiah. This is the historical backdrop as we enter the scene of Isaiah 36.

READ ISAIAH 36:1-22. Describe in your own words the immediate threats Judah faced.

they would be destroyed by the Assyrians

The Assyrian army sent by Sennacherib was "huge" (v. 2). The commander spoke threatening words to incite fear and undermine trust in Yahweh—the God of Israel. He referenced trusting in the Lord seven times (vv. 4-7,9,15) and used these arguments:

- Words won't help you against military might (vv. 4-6);
- God is mad at you for getting rid of His altars (v. 7);
- God called our nation to punish you (v. 10);
- Your leaders can't be trusted because Hezekiah is deceiving you to trust in a God who can't rescue (vv. 14-16);
- Slavery is the best option for you (vv. 16-17);
- Look around you at the other nations we've defeated for evidence that there is no way out (vv. 18-19).

Some of these arguments made by the commander defy logic. He said that God sent them (v. 10) and that God was no match for their power (vv. 18-20). These tactics remind us of those used by another enemy of the Lord. Like the field commander, Satan often uses one argument after another hoping to leave his victims feeling hopeless and helpless. I doubt your attackers have come in the form of physical armies shouting threats, but perhaps your inner dialogue has included some version of these same lies.

> **Read the following statements and put a star next to any that sound familiar, or add another statement related to your own personal battles to trust the Lord.**
>
> - Make a backup plan in case God doesn't come through.
>
> - God is mad at you for messing up so you can't count on Him.
>
> - Your spiritual leaders can't be trusted. They probably have their own agendas.
>
> - Slavery to sin is normal; you'll never overcome these temptations.
>
> - No one else has won these battles so neither will you.
>
> - _____

Lies of the enemy evidence themselves in a variety of ways. When our circumstances feel urgent, waiting on the Lord doesn't always seem like the most prudent posture. So, what should we do during the time between the threat of trouble and God's rescue? Let's go back to the text to see what we can learn from Hezekiah's response to enemy threats.

> **READ ISAIAH 37:1-4.** Identify the responses Hezekiah displayed. What stood out to you from Hezekiah's responses to trouble that you might be able to incorporate in your life?

Hezekiah didn't blame others, negotiate alliances, or seek creature comforts. Instead, he put on scratchy clothes and embraced the gravity of the situation. This was a serious threat. Hezekiah didn't put on a happy face and pretend everything was fine. His faith in God led him to mourn, ask for prayer, and seek God's word through the prophet Isaiah. Hezekiah's example reminds us that trusting God doesn't mean an absence of grief.

READ ISAIAH 37:5-7. Summarize Isaiah's message from the Lord.

Don't be afraid of what you heard from the Assyrians he would put a spirit in him, he would return to his land and fall by the sword in his own land

Isaiah told Hezekiah not to be disturbed by a very disturbing situation. He prophesied that the king of Assyria would return to his land and be killed. Hezekiah then had a choice. He could trust the word of God spoken by Isaiah or strive in human strength to fix the problem. This is often the tension for me. I long to believe God's promises, but I struggle in between the promise and the rescue—especially if that season is prolonged.

My daughter was bald for more than five years. During that time, she worked through her questions and doubts. Sometimes her prayers were raw and full of anguish. Other times they acknowledged God's character and sovereignty in her life. She got to a place where she believed God was good and powerful even if she never had hair. Hezekiah also prayed, holding trouble in one hand but acknowledging God's blessing in another.

"Except for David and Solomon, no king of Judah is given more attention or commendation in Scripture than Hezekiah."[6]

READ ISAIAH 37:15-20. Record in the chart below Hezekiah's praises and requests.

PRAISE (NAMES, CHARACTER, POWER, ETC.)	REQUESTS
Verse 16	Verse 17
Verse 20	Verse 20

For a more in-depth study of Isaiah 37, don't miss the activity sheet "Hezekiah's Prayer," available for free download at lifeway.com/isaiah.

God answered Hezekiah's prayer. Isaiah prophesied against Assyria for the remainder of the chapter. We can trust God in our seasons of waiting, knowing that He is working even when we don't feel it. In between our problem and God's rescue, we can trust more and strive less through prayer. Spend some time considering anywhere your trust feels threatened.

You may not feel like you are facing anything in your life right now like Hezekiah battled. Yet when you learn to trust God with the small things, you will be prepared to trust Him during your own times of crisis. Whether you are facing an aggravation or an atrocity today, pray about it.

Write a two-part prayer, first praising God and then making specific requests.

Praise:

PRAYER

Lord, help me to wait patiently and expectantly. When troubles threaten my trust in You, remind me to pray, seek Your Word, and enlist spiritual support instead of freaking out and planning excessively. I know Your calendar is better than mine. Help me to live that truth when the tyranny of the urgent overwhelms me. In Jesus's name, amen.

Requests:

Hezekiah stayed the course, trusting God even when the situation seemed impossible. He knew that other kingdoms failed against Assyria because their gods weren't real. God sent an angel into "the Assyrian camp and killed 185,000 Assyrian soldiers" (Isa. 37:36). This great loss caused King Sennacherib to return home where his sons killed him with swords while he was worshiping in the temple of his false god Nisroch (v. 38).

God intervened according to His plan, and yet at the same time responded to Hezekiah's prayer. I wonder if Hezekiah would look back on his season of trouble and acknowledge an intimacy with God that desperation can produce. While waiting seasons aren't usually my favorite, they are a place where trust can grow.

DAILY WRAP-UP

MEMORY VERSE

Read Isaiah 30:18 aloud three times. You can find it printed on page 41.

Today we focused on this truth: *In the waiting period between our trouble and God's rescue, we pray.* How would you summarize your personal takeaway from today's study?

Day Two
CHANGING TIMELINES

My prayer habits have always been a struggle. The gap between my desire and actual execution when it comes to prayer confuses me. The open-ended amount of time prayer may take causes me to put it off for later, and too many times later never comes. I recently made some prayer progress by setting alarms on my phone for shorter blocks of prayer throughout the day. Somehow having an end time helps me get started. You may not be wired up like me, but having a system helped my aspirations become more in line with reality.

Use the space below to describe your prayer practices, including both your ideal and your reality:

• What you want your prayer life to look like:

I send up short prayers for the things in the moment. Confessing sin - asking for God to fill my unbeliever family members wt. a spirit be washed over them
Morning

• Your current prayer routines: *all day long*
arrow prayers
then AM + PM but I don't think so deeply in my prayers... I can't comprehend what I need to say

In order to trust God more, we need a fresh vision that prayer changes things—even events on our calendars. Have you ever been confused about Bible verses that say God never changes His mind and then read stories in the Bible where it seemed like He did? Or wondered about the connection between faith and action as you try to walk in God's ways? We'll consider these questions and more as we look at Hezekiah's example today.

SCRIPTURE FOCUS
Isaiah 38

BIG IDEA
Prayer can change even the most established timelines.

Most scholars believe the events of Isaiah 38 and 39 occurred before those in chapters 36 and 37. Some speculate the arrangement has to do with the focus on Assyria in 36 and 37 and Babylon in 38 and 39.[7]

PRAYER FULFILLS GOD'S PLAN.

The account of Hezekiah's sickness and recovery in Isaiah 38:7-8 also appears in 2 Kings 20. We glean an additional detail that Hezekiah was given a choice whether the shadow would move backward or forward in God's sign of the sundial (2 Kings 20:9-11).

"The sundial was probably a pillar whose shadow marked the hours on a double set of stairs."[10]

READ ISAIAH 38:1-8. Briefly describe Hezekiah's sickness and recovery in your own words.

Hezekiah was literally up against a wall. In that moment he likely experienced confusion as well as grief. Hezekiah was from the lineage of David, and he knew God's promise of a descendant of David reigning on the throne of Judah forever (2 Sam. 7:16). Yet he did not have a son at this point in his life.[8] As the leader of a nation, thirty-nine-year-old Hezekiah would have understood the destabilizing affect his absence could bring with no clear succession plan, compounded by threats of Assyrian invasion.[9]

When Hezekiah prayed, the Lord responded to his prayer. This is God's unchanging character and plan. When people humble themselves and pray, He acts! Notice the verbs God used in Isaiah 38:5-6: "I have heard . . . [I have] seen . . . I will add . . . I will rescue . . . I will defend." God not only promised Hezekiah's recovery but also deliverance from Assyria.

Just as the Lord heard Hezekiah's prayers, He also hears ours. God invites us to come boldly before His throne and assures us we will find mercy there (Heb. 4:16). Isaiah 38 and many other examples in Scripture reveal God responding with action to the prayers of His people. We pray because God fulfills His plan of responding to those who seek Him.

While we marvel at this story, it does bring up complicated questions like, *Can prayer change God's mind? If God has a predetermined plan, why pray at all? Why does God answer some prayers and not others?* Although we could spend pages and pages trying to unpack exactly how God's sovereignty and our prayer work together, for now we will leave it at this: We pray because we know God's unchanging character, and because He invites us to ask boldly in faith for anything (Mark 11:24). Throughout Scripture we see that the Lord responds to humble prayers of righteous people (Ex. 32:9-14; 2 Chron. 7:14; Jas. 5:16). The key is to trust Him with the outcome.

One commentator said it this way: God "invites us to tell him what we think our needs are because our trust is deepened as we see God providing the very things we asked for. But that does not mean that we demand he work for us. It means we lay our supposed needs at his feet for him to supply as he sees best. This kind of prayer is no longer an exercise in manipulation. Now it is a conversation between a trusting child and a loving Father."[11]

> If a friend asked, how would you answer the following question: "If God's will is already established, then why should we pray?"

We've navigated some deep prayer waters already, but let's dive back into the chapter for some practical elements of Hezekiah's prayer. We are going to skip to the end of the chapter in order to see what happened next chronologically in the story.

FAITH AND ACTION OFTEN COME TOGETHER IN PRAYER.

> **READ ISAIAH 38:21-22.** What did Isaiah tell the servants to spread over Hezekiah's boil to help him recover (v. 21)? What did Hezekiah ask to prove he would be made well (v. 22)?

Apply a cake of figs
Hezekiah's answer was one the reflected his lack of trust ~ that he needed a sign?

> What do you learn about prayer from these verses?

they can be answered

While a boil may not seem life-threatening to us, some have suggested it was a symptom of leprosy which certainly would have prevented Hezekiah from visiting the temple.[12] Others have proposed a septic ulcer or internal poisoning.[13] No one knows for sure the exact nature of his sickness.

I noticed that praying in faith doesn't mean we don't participate in the answer. Sometimes I have thought that taking action alongside prayer indicated that I didn't trust God to answer. In Hezekiah's story, action went hand in hand with prayer. We can pray for healing and take medicine. We can pray for financial needs and practice good planning. It doesn't have to be one or the other.

Another principle I found in these verses was Hezekiah's desire for a sign. He had faith but also needed reassurance. He models for us the coupling of our human weakness with the power of trusting the Lord. We can believe but ask God to help our unbelief (Mark 9:24). Now let's read Hezekiah's prayer in response to healing in his life.

POWERFUL PRAYERS INCLUDE REFLECTION.

READ ISAIAH 38:9-20. Write down one or two lines of Hezekiah's prayer poem that stand out to you.

Two good examples of parallelism in Hezekiah's poem are Isaiah 38:14, "Like a swallow or a crane I chirp; I moan like a dove," and Isaiah 38:18, "For Sheol does not thank you; death does not praise you" (ESV).

I appreciate how Hezekiah acknowledged the desperation we can experience in prayer when he said, "Delirious, I chattered like a swallow or a crane, and then I moaned like a mourning dove. My eyes grew tired of looking to heaven for help. I am in trouble, Lord. Help me!" (v. 14). Hezekiah reflected on his emotions with authenticity. He didn't try to minimize what he felt.

When my grandmother died in 2020, we weren't able to gather to celebrate her life because of COVID-19 travel restrictions. Typing and organizing her poetry into a keepsake book for our family and friends helped me through my time of grief. She wrote poems throughout her life reflecting on all sorts of milestones. She found beauty in the ordinary and thoughtfully chose her words, meter, and rhyme.

While the Hebrew word used in Isaiah 38:9 for Hezekiah's prayer is *miktab*, which means "writing," many commentators refer to it as a psalm or poem because it parallels the poetic style of a Hebrew lament.[14] The New Living Translation used the word "poem" for *miktab*, likely because of its construction.

Certainly, prayer doesn't have to be poetry, and I'll admit my journal entries look more like stream of consciousness than anything poetic. What Hezekiah's prayer poem reveals to us is that prayer should include reflection, regardless of how poetic it sounds. He took time to consider, practice gratitude, and learn from his experience. He reflected on his thoughts and emotions. I don't think he was rushing an allotted prayer time quota when he wrote, "Lord, your discipline is good, for it leads to life and health. You restore my health and allow me to live! Yes, this anguish was good for me, for you have rescued me from death and forgiven all my sins" (Isa. 38:16-17). Hezekiah helps us know that we don't need desperation to pray. On the other side of trials, we can reflect and praise.

If we really believe prayer changes things, then we won't be so inclined to skip it. We may not understand everything about how prayer works, but I hope Hezekiah's experience inspires us toward greater intensity and regularity in our prayer lives.

> Let's take a few moments to do that now. Reflect on your relationship with the Lord. Use the acrostic PRAY to write four lines to the Lord, starting each sentence with a word beginning with these letters:

Praise to you - your souvernity, grace, love

R

A

Y

DAILY WRAP-UP

> Today we focused on this truth: *Prayer can change even the most established timelines.* How would you summarize your personal takeaway from today's study?

PRAYER

Lord, I believe but help my unbelief. Leaving outcomes in Your hands sounds so good but I struggle to do it. I want to ask expectantly but also trust Your answers. Please show me what action to take as I seek Your help. Thank You for inviting me to come to You and for being merciful to me. I want to reflect more on Your power and goodness in my life through prayer. In Jesus's name, amen.

MEMORY VERSE

Read Isaiah 30:18 aloud one time. Then write it down in your book or on a separate piece of paper.

Day Three

A LONG-TERM MINDSET

**SCRIPTURE
FOCUS**
Isaiah 39

BIG IDEA
Trust is intended to
be a way of life, not
an antidote for crisis.

When my friend Lee was first diagnosed with a brain tumor in his
thirties, he encountered a spiritual awakening that drew him into
a season of intense intimacy with the Lord. After extensive surgery,
recovery, and grueling treatments, doctors declared him cancer-free.
I met Lee shortly after his recovery, and our families became close
friends. I'll never forget a remark he made about his experience while
we were at a church campout. He told me that as crazy as it sounded, he
missed the desperation that drew him so close to Jesus. "Don't get me
wrong," he said. "I don't want my cancer back, but I find myself slipping
back into caring too much about things that don't really matter." His
cancer gave him a clarity about life that made temporal concerns about
things like jobs, money, houses, or slight offenses lose their luster when
compared with eternal realities. Lee fought against the slippery slope into
self-reliance and overconfidence that can develop on the other side of
a great work of God in our lives.

Today's chapter hints
toward events that
will occur more than
one hundred years
into Judah's future
of Babylonian exile,
which occurred
in 586 BC.[15]

**You may not have had cancer like Lee or been healed
from a terminal disease like Hezekiah, but I wonder if
you can think of a season when you experienced God's
nearness in your life. Write down anything that comes
to mind.** The death of my parents

So far, we've been inspired by Hezekiah's trust in the Lord and poetic
prayers. In Isaiah 39, we will uncover his mistake in failing to maintain
a long-term mindset. After a supernatural healing, he wasn't careful
in considering how his decisions would impact the future. We will be
reminded afresh today that a long-term mindset impacts short-term
decisions. Isaiah teaches us that trust in God should be a lifelong
expression rather than a means of getting out of crisis.

AVOID DISTRACTIONS

READ ISAIAH 39:1-8. What country did Merodach-baladan reign over as king? Why did he send an envoy and a gift to Hezekiah (v. 1)?

> The Babylonians created the sun dial and worshiped a sun god.

What was Hezekiah's response to the envoy arriving (v. 2)?

What questions did Isaiah ask Hezekiah, and how did Hezekiah respond (vv. 3-4)?

> "The LORD Almighty," the title for God used by Isaiah in verse 5 of the NIV, "lays emphasis on the infinite resources used by the Lord in his acts of power. Hezekiah's own resources may have seemed great to him, but those of the Lord were far greater."[16]

What did Isaiah prophesy would happen, and what was Hezekiah's response to the prophecy (vv. 5-8)?

The letters sent by the king of Babylon likely contained a hidden agenda. He wanted Hezekiah to join him in the fight against Assyria. The Lord had already assured Hezekiah of rescue from Assyria (Isa. 38:6). Hezekiah could have responded to the letters and the envoy politely, sharing with them the power of God and His promise to save them.

Instead, Hezekiah seemed to be enthralled with the attention. When Isaiah asked him questions to give him an opportunity to see his error, Hezekiah responded about the men coming from distant lands. One commentator surmised his reaction as, "Imagine them coming all that way to see me! Imagine Merodach-Baladan wanting me as an ally!"[17] While we can't assume Hezekiah's exact thoughts, we do know that after the Lord healed him, he became self-absorbed instead of trusting the Lord (Isa. 39:2).

AVOID SHORT-SIGHTEDNESS

READ 2 CHRONICLES 32:24-31. Write down two or three additional insights we find from this complementary passage.

In your opinion, what was wrong with Hezekiah's mindset at this time in his life?

You might say Hezekiah didn't focus on the Lord and the future impact of his decisions. He was living in the moment possibly with pride, overconfidence, and forgetfulness of God's sovereign plan. The Lord healed him and promised to protect the nation, but when the urgent crisis ended, Hezekiah seemed to get caught up in his possessions. Isaiah's questions were meant to help him see his trust in man rather than God for protection. Yet Hezekiah responded by being defensive instead of humble.

When Isaiah told Hezekiah his wealth and some of his own sons would be carried away into captivity by the very nation allowed to inspect his possessions, how did his response reveal his short-sightedness?

We get a glimpse into Hezekiah's mindset in Isaiah 39:8b, "For the king was thinking, 'At least there will be peace and security during my lifetime.'" Again, he was thinking only of his personal pain for the moment. Avoiding pain is our human nature, but Hezekiah's concern for himself reveals his lack of foresight. He didn't grieve for his offspring or seem too concerned about his legacy but instead reveled in his own comfort.

ADOPT A LONG-TERM MINDSET

We want to develop a long-term mindset that impacts our short-term decisions so we can avoid falling into the overconfidence of Hezekiah. We don't only want to trust the Lord when things are dire in our lives. Instead, we want to make trusting the Lord a way of life that guides us in good times and on difficult days. Let's practice this together.

Make a short list of decisions you will make today and in the future. (These can be as simple as what you will eat or what you post on social media or more significant things like finding a church or leaving a job. Try to include a mix of small and big decisions in your responses.)

TODAY	THIS WEEK	IN THE COMING MONTHS

Now look back over what you've written and put a star by the one that weighs most heavily on you—whether it's a daily choice or a one-time decision. Consider the impact of your choice in one month, one year, ten years, and even into eternity. How might taking a long-term mindset influence the choice you marked?

If this is hard to answer, let me give some examples: *How might the decision to pray regularly or not pray regularly impact your spiritual growth? How might your daily food decisions affect your long-term health? How might spending more or less time at work influence your family life?*

PRAYER

Lord, I don't want to get stuck in the moment. Help me to seek You whether I have a desperate need, a great blessing, or the in-between mundane. I know my tendency to drift away from trusting You and striving in my own strength. As I make decisions today, tomorrow, and into the future, help me consider You in each one. In Jesus's name, amen.

MEMORY VERSE

Write down Isaiah 30:18. Also record one thought you have as you read over this verse.

Taking a long-term mindset is recognized even in secular circles. Brian Tracy wrote in his book *Eat That Frog*, "Your attitude toward time, your 'time horizon,' has an enormous impact on your behavior and your choices. People who take a long-term view of their lives and careers seem to make much better decisions about their time and activities than people who give very little thought to the future."[18] If only Hezekiah could have maintained a "time horizon" with eternity in mind, he likely would have thanked the Babylonians for their well-wishes and turned again to the Lord to sustain him.

Having a long-term mindset impacts our lives here on earth, but it also reflects the heart of the gospel message. Believing that Jesus came to reconcile us to the Father because of our sin stretches us to think not just about today but about what will matter in eternity. Jesus taught us to look beyond the externals like food and clothing to the eternal. We may not have a prophet like Isaiah confronting us with questions specific to our decision making, but the words of the Lord still align us to a long-term mindset in the pages of Scripture!

DAILY WRAP-UP

Today we focused on this truth: *Trust is intended to be a way of life, not an antidote for crisis.* **How would you summarize your personal takeaway from today's study?**

Day Four

THE POWER OF REFLECTION

When it comes to calendars, I like to have a month at a glance so I can see the broad strokes of my schedule. I always buy a planner that also has weekly pages so I can flesh out each day more meticulously with meeting times, deadlines, and my daily to-do list. Depending on your personality type, you may not be as attached to your calendar as I am, but all of us need a system for keeping track of life.

What type of planner, calendar, or digital resource are you currently using to organize your days?

No matter how you manage your time, most of us would admit we struggle to trust God's calendar. The Lord calls us to plan wisely (Ps. 90:12). We all must make decisions about our routines and time commitments including work, rest, relationships, hobbies, social media, and so on. On the other hand, we all know that our best laid plans often get hijacked by emergencies, unforeseen circumstances, or even global pandemics!

As we endeavor to trust God's calendar, we need wisdom to discern what to pencil into ours. Isaiah's message gives us practical insights that will help us make plans while holding them loosely in anticipation of divine interventions.

REMEMBER ~~WHAT GOD HAS DONE IN THE PAS~~T.

READ ISAIAH 46. **How long did God say He has cared for His people?**

How long did God say He would care for them (vv. 3-4)?

> **SCRIPTURE FOCUS**
> Isaiah 46; 47; 51

> **BIG IDEA**
> Remember what the Lord has done in the past so you can trust Him in the present.

> Proverbs 16:9 reminds us, "We can make our plans, but the LORD determines our steps."

> "All references so far made in the prophecy of Isaiah to pagan deities or idols have been general. Here, Isaiah named the two great gods of Babylon: Bel (also called Marduk) and Nebo."[19]

What command did God issue regarding the past (vv. 8-9)?

What did the Lord remind them about the future (v. 10)?

Notice how the gods of Babylon had to be carried (v. 1), but the Lord said He would carry His people (v. 4). Isaiah used this play on words to remind his readers that idols were man-made objects. They weren't real. Without intentional remembering, we can also get swept into the superficial thinking of our culture. What we believe will drive how we prioritize our time. The Lord challenged His people to remember what He had done in the past so they would trust Him instead of worthless counterfeits.

These reminders weren't intended only for the original audience. The Lord also calls us to remember His work in our own stories.

> Fill in the bullet points below with ways the Lord has cared for you in the past. These don't have to be major moments. Try to think of times God provided, comforted, spoke, or affirmed even in small ways.
>
> •
>
> •
>
> •

Hezekiah could have recalled how the Lord gave him fifteen more years of life or how the people living in Judah were saved from the Assyrian army. Your list might not feel as dramatic, but some of your marked moments might include protection from harm, comfort during a season of grief, encouragement when you needed it most, or something totally different.

REFLECT ON CHOICES IN THE PRESENT.

When we remember what the Lord has done in our lives in the past, it can help us trust Him today. God not only foretold of Babylon's victory over Judah but also their ultimate fall.

> **READ ISAIAH 47:1-10.** Make notes of the charges the Lord laid against Babylon.

"Most commentators consider chapter 47 to be a self-contained poem."[20]

Babylon showed Judah "no mercy" (v. 6). They loved pleasure and felt secure in their wickedness (vv. 8,10). They relied on their own wisdom and knowledge, which led them astray (v. 10). We will hit some of these themes later in our study of Isaiah, but for our purposes today, we will focus on verse 7b.

> **READ ISAIAH 47:7b** in the following four translations. Circle all the words that begin with the letter R.

You did not reflect on your actions
or think about their consequences (NLT).

But you did not consider these things
or reflect on what might happen (NIV).

So that you did not lay these things
to heart or remember their end (ESV).

These things you did not consider
Nor remember the outcome of them (NASB).

We want to remember what God has done in the past, but we also need to reflect on our choices in the present. The Lord punished Babylon for acting thoughtlessly. He calls us to pause in the midst of our busy days to think about what we are doing, why we are doing it, and how it will impact others.

Look at your calendar or planner right now. Glance over the next seven days and take some time to reflect on these questions:

How are you planning to spend your time in the coming week?

What interruptions might you anticipate?

Is there anything you sense the Lord would add or eliminate from your agenda?

After your time of reflection, write down any insights, ideas, or questions in the space provided.

Isaiah wrote all these prophecies more than one hundred years before the Babylonian exile began, and the prophet Jeremiah foretold the time frame of seventy years for the captivity (Jer. 29:10).

I've found that taking just five or ten minutes to stop, pray, and remember what I'm doing and why I'm doing it has been so helpful. You may employ other methods of reflection, but all of us can heed the Lord's call to think more deeply. When Jesus was accused of breaking the Sabbath (by healing of all things), He challenged people not to get caught in the shallow end of God's plan. He ended His teaching with these words, "Look beneath the surface so you can judge correctly" (John 7:24). This command summarizes God's message through Isaiah regarding reflecting on our actions. God wants us to be mindful of living for Him rather than just going through the motions of Christianity.

REAFFIRM GOD'S GOODNESS FOR THE FUTURE.

The Lord not only calls us to remember the past and reflect on the present but also to look toward the future. A future with God is a future with hope. God entrusted Isaiah with details of the Babylonian exile, punishment, and return. Isaiah also gave the people glimpses of God's future goodness to them. Whether we are in the midst of a season of prosperity or desperation, we can all look to the future with anticipation.

> **READ ISAIAH 51:9-16.** Fill in the blanks with a one-word answer to complete each sentence regarding the future for God's people as recorded in verse 11. (I've used the NLT Bible version.)
>
> "Those who have been ransomed [rescued, redeemed] by the LORD will _____. They will enter Jerusalem [Zion] _____, crowned with everlasting _____. Sorrow and mourning will _____, and they will be filled with joy and gladness."

Before the future captivity would unfold, the Lord wanted the people to know ahead of time that He would rescue them. He gave them a peek at His divine calendar so they could be prepared, but also so they could trust Him through the process. However, like many of us, the Israelites quickly forgot about God's past faithfulness, present power, and future promises.

The Lord's accusation against them was forgetfulness. He reminded them that He had stretched out the sky like a canopy and laid the foundations of the earth in times past (v. 13). Then He spoke of His present power as the Lord who "stirs up the sea, causing its waves to roar" (v. 15). God told them what they could expect in the future so they would know they belonged to Him, "the LORD of Heaven's Armies" (v. 15).

You may or may not be of Jewish descent, but if you have turned from your sin and turned to God, then you belong to Him. What we glean from Isaiah's words is the importance of trusting God's calendar. We remember the past, reflect in the present, and reaffirm the future hope in God's good plans for our lives.

When you attach your trust to God's eternal blessings rather than ease, convenience, and trouble-free circumstances here on earth, you can more easily surrender your calendar to His control. Things may be written in your planner that you didn't anticipate. I know you didn't write *cancer, divorce,* a *breakup,* or a *miscarriage* into your schedule.

God longs to walk with you through each and every day, whether it is marked with difficulty or celebration.

Today's passages helped me to process through the tension I feel between these two statements:

- God calls me to plan wisely.
- God calls me to trust His plan.

I believe we reconcile both of these truths as we loosen our grip on our own agendas. Reflection doesn't come naturally for me, but I want to grow in remembering, considering the impact of my decisions, and smiling at the future. I'm asking the Lord to show me how to implement reflection in my life, and I hope He is stirring your heart as well.

DAILY WRAP-UP

Today we focused on this truth: *Remember what the Lord has done in the past so you can trust Him in the present.* How would you summarize your personal takeaway from today's study?

PRAYER

Lord, I can be controlling with my calendar. Help me to surrender it to You. Show me what it looks like to plan well but hold my agenda loosely. I want to see Your interventions as opportunities rather than interruptions to my schedule. Give me a healthy view of my past and help me pause reflectively in my present decisions so that I don't fail to consider You in all things. In Jesus's name, amen.

MEMORY VERSE

Attempt to write out Isaiah 30:18 from memory, then check to see how you did.

Day Five

WRITTEN ON HIS PALM

The school called yesterday to let me know my son had been waiting in the office for ten minutes. I had remembered to write the note to excuse him from school for an appointment, but I lost track of time while answering emails and plugging through my to-do list. I sure hope you can relate! I set alarms on my phone, write lists in my planner, and still struggle to remember things.

In our study today, we'll find that thankfully the Lord doesn't have this same struggle. He has never forgotten anything, ever—except that He chooses to forget about our sin (Isa. 43:25). It may feel like He doesn't always respond to our prayers or intervene when we think He should, but He's never early or late and certainly has not forgotten about us.

Just like I sometimes forget appointments, I also forget about God's perfect timing. I hope reading Isaiah 49 will remind you of the Lord's faithfulness and help you trust His timing when it comes to the details of your life. If He knew just the right moment to send His Son into the world, I know you can trust Him with your calendar as well!

THE SERVANT MESSIAH

Before we dig into the passage, I want to give us some background information. In the chapters leading up to chapter 49, Isaiah prophesied regarding Israel's exile to Babylon and the fall of Babylon to King Cyrus of Persia. Isaiah called Cyrus by name 170 years before he invaded Babylon (Isa. 44:28).[21] Some have used this prophetic detail to question the date and authorship of Isaiah by wondering how the prophet could have known these specifics about Cyrus and the rise of the Persian Empire. However, these references provide no problem for those of us who believe Isaiah's writings to be a divine work inspired by a supernatural God who sits outside of time and knows all things.

SCRIPTURE FOCUS
Isaiah 49

BIG IDEA
We can trust God's timing because He sent His Son, Jesus, just as He promised.

Isaiah contains four Servant Songs found in Isaiah 42:1-4; 49:1-6; 50:4-11; and 52:13–53:12. Each one makes reference to the Servant of the Lord, whom we know as Jesus, the promised Messiah. These passages highlight the Messiah's role as a Suffering Servant rather than a conquering king.

In chapter 49, the language shifts from describing a human king to giving Messianic references. Isaiah spoke of One who would come to rescue not just God's people but the entire world!

READ ISAIAH 49:1-7. Circle the multiple-choice letter that best answers each question.

1. Whom does the Lord's servant address in verse 1?
   A. Those who live in Judah
   B. The Babylonians
   C. All those living far away (islands, coastlands)

2. What was the servant's commission in verses 5-6?
   A. To bring Israel back to the Lord
   B. To be a light to the Gentiles and bring salvation to the ends of the earth
   C. Both A and B

3. How is the servant described in regard to the nations in verse 7?
   A. Royal and stately *where does it read that*
   B. Forgetful and lazy
   C. Trendy and cool

In what ways does the servant in these verses remind you of Jesus?

I will make you the light of the nations so my salvation may reach to the end of the earth

READ THE FOLLOWING COMPLEMENTARY PASSAGES and circle any words or phrases that remind you of Isaiah 49:1-7.

He is a light to reveal God to the nations,
and he is the glory of your people Israel!
LUKE 2:32 (prophesied by Simeon at Christ's birth)

> "The Jewish nation was called to glorify God and be a light to the Gentiles, but they failed in their mission. This is why Messiah is called 'Israel' in Isaiah 49:3: He did the work that Israel was supposed to do."[22]

For the Lord gave us this command when he said,
"I have made you a light to the Gentiles, to bring
salvation to the farthest corners of the earth."
ACTS 13:47 (Paul preaching the gospel to Gentiles)

He was despised and rejected—a man of sorrows,
acquainted with deepest grief. We turned our backs on him
and looked the other way. He was despised, and we did not care.
ISAIAH 53:3 (Isaiah writing a messianic prophecy)

Through Isaiah, the Redeemer of Israel told His people about their future rescue from exile in Babylon, but He also hinted at a much greater fulfillment that would come centuries later when Jesus came to earth in human form to die for our sins. None of the original audience would live long enough to see the exile or rescue of God's people—or even the birth of Christ. Yet God revealed glimpses so they could see His design and live with hope and trust in Him.

THE SHEPHERD MESSIAH

READ ISAIAH 49:8-26. When did the Lord say He would respond (v. 8)? in a day of salvation

What would He say to the prisoners? What would He say to those in darkness (v. 9)? Those in darkness - show yourself. Prisoners - go forth

What did Jerusalem (or Zion) say, and how did the Lord respond (vv. 14-15)? The Lord has forsaken me + forgotten me. I will not forget you

What has the Lord written on the palms of His hands (v. 16)? He has inscribed you on my hands - Your walls are continually before me

What will the people and the nations know after all this happens (vv. 23,26)? Know that I am (Messiah) am the LORD vs 23 26 I the LORD am your SAVIOR, REDEEMER, The Mighty One of Jacob

What illustrations or word pictures stood out to you from these promises?

In this poetic Servant Song, we find the Lord using illustrations of a shepherd leading his people beside cool water, a nursing mother never forgetting her child, a courageous warrior, and a God who has written our names in the palm of His hand. Jesus is the Shepherd who leaves the ninety-nine to go after the one lost sheep (Matt. 18:12-14). Jesus is the Son, but He also takes the role of a compassionate mother caring for a dependent child. Jesus may be tender, but He is not weak. The Lord said, "I will fight those who fight you, and I will save your children" (Isa. 49:25b).

All of these pictures remind us of God's incredible love for His people, but the one image that really tugs at my emotions is God's engraving of our names in the palm of His hand. Pastor Warren Wiersbe said, "The word *engraved* means 'to cut into' signifying its permanence."[23] This writing wasn't something like a pencil, pen, or even a Sharpie® marker; it was a permanent signature, often chiseled in stone. Take a minute to let that sink in. These verses were not just for the nation of Israel. Yahweh is not the God of the Jews but the God of the entire world. This means He knows your name. He knows what you are waiting for. He understands the questions going through your mind right now.

Sometimes when I'm thinking, I like to doodle. As you ponder these truths, take a moment to write your name in the palm below.

God is faithful to do what He says He will do at just the right time. He sent His Servant, Jesus, to save us from our sin. His hand is extended toward us. Our memory verse said it so well this week.

Reread this verse again and underline what God is waiting to show you:

So the LORD must wait for <u>you to come to him</u> so he can show you <u>his love and compassion.</u> For the LORD is a faithful God. Blessed are those who wait for his help.

ISAIAH 30:18

The Lord isn't waiting to punish us; He's waiting to show us His love and compassion. He's waiting for us to come to Him, and He says we are blessed when we wait for His help. The apostle Paul referenced Isaiah 49:8 when he wrote a letter to the church at Corinth. He said, "For God says, 'At just the right time, I heard you. On the day of salvation, I helped you.' Indeed, the 'right time' is now. Today is the day of salvation" (2 Cor. 6:2).

If you have never confessed with your mouth and believed in your heart that Jesus is the Messiah, today is the day! For those of you who have embraced this truth already, perhaps today is a fresh reminder of God's perfect timing. Even when we can't see or feel it, <u>God works out</u> His <u>perfect plan in His perfect timing.</u> If God sent Jesus at just the right time, then we can trust His timing for the events in our lives.

Take a few minutes to write out a prayer, thanking God for His perfect timing in your life.

Lord God - I know my timing is all about my will - I let my desires + wishes become the center of my thoughts. But I know I must not act on my own but wait for your perfect timing in my life. Thank you Lord for putting me on the right path and help me wait

DAILY WRAP-UP

Today we focused on this truth: *We <u>can trust</u> God's timing because He sent His Son, Jesus, just as He* (promised.) **How would you summarize your personal takeaway from today's study?**

I is all about My will not His will - I must be patient and the Lord will let me know his timing - maybe by opening a door for me that was closed

God, thank You for sending Your Son, the despised and rejected Servant who brought light into my life! It blows my mind to think that my name is written in the palm of Your hand. Give me patience to be a better waiter. Help me to trust that Your faithful timing is best. In Jesus's name, amen.

MEMORY VERSE

Write down or say aloud Isaiah 30:18 from memory.

Session Three
VIDEO VIEWER GUIDE

To access the video teaching sessions, use the instructions in the back of your Bible study book.

Realigning to God's _____ leads us to trust His _____.

Waiting can feel like a _____ of _____ (Isa. 36:4-5).

The _____ _____ _____ and _____ help us get off the wheel of worry (Isa. 37:6-7,14-22).

What doesn't seem like a _____ can often be the most _____.

> So the LORD must _*wait*_ for you to come to him
> so he can show you his love and compassion.
> For the LORD is a faithful God.
> Blessed are those who _*wait long*_ for his help.
> Isaiah 30:18, NLT

WOW: _*God*_____

_____

WOE: _*get of the hamster wheel*_____

_____

_____

ACTION STEP: Be _*present*_ in your presence.

Session Three
GROUP DISCUSSION GUIDE

SHARE: What is something you're looking forward to that is coming up on your calendar?

WATCH the video "Session Three: Trust God's Calendar" (29:18 minutes) together and follow along with the viewer guide on the previous page.

MEMORY VERSE
Review Isaiah 30:18 and give the group an opportunity to recite it aloud.

VIDEO DISCUSSION
1. *Ask:* How have waiting and worry felt like a mental hamster wheel in your life?
2. *Discuss:* What two things can help us get off the wheel of worry? Describe a time when this was true for you.

STUDY DISCUSSION
1. Call for a volunteer to read aloud Isaiah 37:1-4. Ask women to share how they answered this question on page 44: *What stood out to you from Hezekiah's responses to trouble that you might be able to incorporate in your life?*
2. Ask your group to share their responses to the Day Two opening question to describe the gap between their desires in prayer and their current prayer routines (p. 47). Together encourage one another by sharing ways God has answered prayer.
3. Guide women to describe how they answered the Day Three Daily Wrap-Up question (p. 56): *How would you summarize your personal takeaway from today's study?*
4. Review the three subtitles from Day Four: *Remember What God Has Done in the Past* (Isa. 46); *Reflect on Choices in the Present* (Isa. 47:1-10); *Reaffirm God's Goodness for the Future* (Isa. 51:9-16). Choose one of these passages to read and discuss together as a group.
5. Ask someone to read Isaiah 49:8-26 out loud. Discuss what stood out from these verses regarding our ability to trust the Lord in waiting seasons.

REVIEW
Review the Big Idea for each of the five days of study. Ask for final thoughts or questions regarding the study of God's calendar from Isaiah this week.

PRAYER REQUESTS
Share prayer requests and lead your group to record them on the tops of the starting pages for each day of study for the coming week (Session Four). When they open their books each day, they can begin each day of study by praying for others in their group.

TRUST *God's* COMFORT

SESSION FOUR

Trusting God's comfort when I'm weary, sad, or experiencing pain or crisis can be challenging. Instead, I want to numb and delay my discomfort. I don't feel like praying—I feel like watching television and eating ice cream. These aren't inherently sinful comforts, but they don't offer the restorative comfort God longs to give us. Isaiah will help us discover that God extends His hand toward us. He doesn't crush us when we are weak; rather, He longs to renew our strength and walk with us through the trials and difficulties we face. He sent Jesus to bring us comfort and support in the moments we need it most. In the passages of Scripture we will study this week, Isaiah will teach us what it looks like to respond to God's offer of true comfort through deeper trust in Him.

MEMORY VERSE

But those who trust in the LORD will find new strength. They will soar high on wings like eagles. They will run and not grow weary. They will walk and not faint.

ISAIAH 40:31

Day One

COMFORT FOR THE WEARY

SCRIPTURE FOCUS

Isaiah 40

BIG IDEA

When we trust in the Lord, He comforts us with new strength and energy.

I left the Zoom® meeting and raced out of the house hoping to stop at Target® and pick up a gift to bring to my lunch appointment. As I sped into the store, I got a call from my caseworker who wanted to discuss some concerns regarding our foster son, so I talked with her while getting what I needed and driving downtown. The only parking I could find was at a meter that required me to download an app and enter payment information. Whatever happened to good old quarters in a meter? I completed the task, slammed the car door, and began walking to the restaurant. Then it hit me, I forgot to grab a mask! Since this happened during the COVID-19 mask mandates, I couldn't enter the establishment without one. As I ran back to the car, I searched my pockets for my key. It wasn't there. I peeked into my vehicle and saw it—sitting on the passenger seat. After my husband brought me a spare key, I arrived at our house exhausted physically, emotionally, and mentally. I'll bet you've had days like this too.

When was the last time you can remember feeling weary, and what were the circumstances (whether physical, emotional, mental, or spiritual) that contributed to your exhaustion?

The prophecies found in Isaiah 40 were meant to encourage and comfort God's people during the Babylonian exile. His message addressed events that would happen more than 150 years after Isaiah's day.[1]

When days like that happen, all I want are my favorite creature comforts— watching television, eating ice cream, changing into my pajamas, and checking out for the rest of the day. Today as we open the pages of Isaiah, we will find that trusting God's comfort includes discerning where to turn in our exhaustion. Sure, God gave us comfort foods. Hobbies can distract us from our weariness. Talking to a good friend can provide consolation. The Lord can use these things to comfort us. Yet at other times, we comfort ourselves with methods of escape that aren't necessarily healthy. Isaiah often addressed God's desire to comfort His people. Today, we will explore what it looks like to trust God instead of our counterfeit comforts when we feel weary.

THE OFFER TO COMFORT

READ ISAIAH 40:1-11. What repeated word did God say over His people (v. 1)?

What illustration did Isaiah use to contrast the permanence of God's words (vv. 7-8)?

What profession did Isaiah use to describe how the Lord will care for His people (v. 11)?

I love the picture of the Lord leading the mother sheep with her young. He is the shepherd feeding and caring tenderly for His flock. He has the "powerful arm" to strike (v. 10), but He uses that same arm to carry His lambs (v. 11). Isaiah revealed the Lord as a "strong and tender Shepherd-King."[2]

God's message of comfort wasn't only for those in Isaiah's day. In the midst of these tender expressions is a reminder that God's words aren't like withering grass or fading flowers. These words of God last forever; they apply to us today!

As you consider your own weary seasons, how have you experienced God's comfort through tender words or shepherding care? Write briefly about a situation that comes to mind.

Shepherds provide, protect, and sometimes carry their lambs. God has been my Shepherd on frenetic days like the one I mentioned earlier, but also in seasons of grief, difficult circumstances, and spiritual fatigue. I remember weary seasons of parenting small children and tough ministry seasons when I felt betrayed by close friends. God longs to comfort us, but we must come to Him rather than seek to comfort ourselves.

THE AUTHORITY TO COMFORT

READ ISAIAH 40:12-26. Draw a line to the correct word to complete the sentences below:

Verse 12: God measured (and holds in His hands) . . .

the stars.

Verse 15: The nations of the world are like . . .

the circle of the earth.

Verses 18-19: God cannot be compared with . . .

a drop in a bucket, dust on a scale.

Verse 22: God sits above . . .

images and idols.

Verse 26: God created and knows by name . . .

the oceans (waters) and heavens.

Of these descriptions of God's power and might, what stood out most to you?

Why would you guess that Isaiah took so much time to establish God's credibility?

Since God's people turned to counterfeit comforts, I wonder if Isaiah reminded them of God's position and power as the One to console them in their pain. He knows the name of every star (v. 26), and He knows your name as well. The same God who numbers and names the stars longs to comfort you in your seasons of weariness and heartbreak. When you see God clearly, you can trust Him with your trials. He wants you to believe by faith that He is present and powerful in your pain.

READ ISAIAH 40:27-31. Record the questions the Lord asked of Israel in verse 27.

Jacob's name became Israel after he wrestled with God (Gen. 32:28). The Lord used both his names here as He spoke to the entire nation regarding their complaint that He ignored their troubles. The people brought God down to their level by thinking of Him as weary or forgetful. We can also be in danger of reducing our magnificent God with human frailties. Many of us can relate to doubts about the Lord seeing or intervening during our times of distress whether we would admit it out loud or not. Isaiah used these questions to remind them of God's character: "Have you never heard? Have you never understood?" (Isa. 40:28). Notice the repetition of these questions in chapter 40—they are the same ones Isaiah asked in verse 21! In essence he was saying, "Don't you know who your God really is?"

In your own words, describe the reminders about God's ability to care for His people found in verses 28-29.

God is the everlasting Creator of the whole earth. He doesn't get weary like we do, and the depths of His understanding can't be measured. The Hebrew word for *weary* can be defined as "failure through loss of inherent strength," and the word *tired* as "pointing to exhaustion because of the hardness of life."[3] We can relate to these definitions in our humanness, but the Lord never loses strength or gets exhausted. Instead, He gives us power when we are weak.

THE BENEFITS OF COMFORT

In the last verse in this chapter (Isa. 40:31, which is also our memory verse for this week), we find a conditional promise. What condition is given for finding new strength, soaring high like eagles, running without getting weary, and walking without growing faint?

Depending on your translation you might have said *trusting, waiting,* or *hoping.* These are different interpretations for the Hebrew word *qavah,* which means "to wait, look for, hope, expect."[4] If we are trusting, waiting, and hoping in the Lord, our counterfeit comforts will lose their luster. Waiting on the Lord isn't just sitting around doing nothing; it means living in a posture of hopeful expectation of His help.

What helps you trust, wait, and hope in the Lord in weary seasons?

PRAYER

Lord, You are the everlasting God, the Creator of heaven and earth. I'm so glad You never grow tired of my constant need for Your strength. I get frustrated and weary often, and I need You. Help me to remember how big You are—especially in my moments of fatigue when I think temporary distractions are the answer. In Jesus's name, amen.

MEMORY VERSE ACTIVITY

Read Isaiah 40:31 aloud three times. You can find it printed on page 71.

Isaiah makes a case that it isn't duty but delight to trust God's comfort. When we understand that God longs to walk alongside us through the difficulties of life on a broken planet, we can take delight in simply walking this road with Him. As we look for takeaways from Isaiah 40, the last thing we want to do is strive against creature comforts. Instead, we embrace a bigger vision of God as the One who is able to give us strength.

When we believe these truths wholeheartedly, we're inspired rather than guilted into trusting God more. We don't want to swat at our bad habits but rather enlarge our view of the Lord so that it deepens our belief. This is how we move from surface-level behavior modification to heart-level transformation. When you have a weary day or season, I pray you will wait on the Lord to renew your strength. He knows all about long meetings, unexpected phone calls, keys locked in cars, and the more significant losses and frustrations that lead to your exhaustion. He calls you to wait on Him for the power and strength you'll never find in your own striving.

DAILY WRAP-UP

Today we focused on this truth: *When we trust in the Lord, He comforts us with new strength and energy.* How would you summarize your personal takeaway from today's study?

Day Two

COMFORT IN HOLDING THE RIGHT HAND

I reached out my right hand as I had so many times before. She took it and squeezed hard. Even though my daughter is now a college student, she still likes a hand to hold when she gets injections in her scalp during her ongoing battle with alopecia. Sometimes, we all need a hand to hold. Life can be scary, and our Creator knows it well.

When I experience grief or stress because of real circumstances or hypothetical fears, I long for something to provide relief, and a person's hand to hold doesn't always do the trick. To alleviate the pressure of overthinking or overwhelming sadness, I often look for a quick fix. Studies show that a chemical in our brain called dopamine gets released when we take a bite of delicious food, interact on social media, check email, or during other pleasurable activities. Dopamine plays a part in why people struggle with addiction. We are wired to repeat behaviors that bring us short-term pleasure.[5]

In today's passage, the Lord makes a case for choosing His help over counterfeit comforts. He wants us to reach for His hand rather than rely on fakes, which in the Bible were often idols. The idolatry of Isaiah's day included craftsmen making objects to be worshiped. We might read these passages with a sigh of relief because we don't physically bow before man-made statues. But idolatry didn't go out of style—it just looks a little different in modern culture.

CONSIDER THE JUDGE

READ ISAIAH 41:1-7. **What legal language do you find in verse 1? What do we learn about God in these verses?**

SCRIPTURE FOCUS

Isaiah 41

BIG IDEA

God offers His hand of help, but we must turn away from counterfeits in order to receive His comfort.

"Just as God says here, 'I am he' (41:4), so Jesus said, 'I am he' (John 8:58; 18:5)."[6]

Isaiah prophesied that a king "from the east" (v. 2) would come to conquer many nations. That sounds scary as I think about how much I value safety for my own family. I wouldn't want to hear that war and destruction would be a part of my children and grandchildren's futures. Most modern commentators agree this is a reference to Cyrus, a king of Persia who would conquer Babylon and eventually allow the people of Judah to return home after seventy years of exile.[7] Isaiah described Cyrus more than a century before he was born.[8] God is "the First and the Last" (v. 4), so He could easily tell Isaiah about a person who would rule in the future.

> **List a couple of specific things in these two categories that you are encouraged to know God is the First and Last (sovereign) over:**
>
> • **Current world events:**
>
>
>
> • **Your own personal circumstances:**

As we see the Lord intervene in history, we remember that He is well aware of all that is happening in our world today. He is the First and Last—the blessed Controller of all things. Even when He allows discipline or hardship, He offers His help and comfort.

Isaiah also predicted that the people of the world would strengthen their idols and encourage each other to be strong (vv. 6-7). God warned His own people not to hold hands with idols or even put their sole trust in each other to get them through the scary season of Persia's domination. Instead, He reminded them to reach for their Creator's hand.

CONSIDER HIS OFFER

> READ ISAIAH 41:8-14. Fill in the blanks with God's promises of help in the following verses. (Using the NLT Bible version helps with this exercise.)
>
> Verse 9: "I have called you back from the ends of the earth."
>
> I have _____.
> I will not _____.

Verse 10: I am with _____.

I am your _____.
I will _____ you and _____ you.
I will hold you with my _____.

Verse 11: Anyone who opposes you will _____
_____.

Verse 13: I hold you by your right _____.
I am here to _____.

Verse 14: I will _____ you.
My names are _____.

God knows our futures just as He knew the future for Isaiah's original audience. It included some difficulty (war, famine, and exile) but also a return to their homeland. God called His people to hold His hand through the highs and lows of their circumstances. We must choose whether to hold hands with the things we can touch, taste, and feel or to reach out in faith to clasp God's outstretched arm.

CONSIDER THE POSSIBILITIES

READ ISAIAH 41:15-20. Fill in the chart below completing "You will" and "I will" statements from the verses (I filled in one for you so you get the idea.):

"YOU WILL"	"I WILL"
Verse 15	Verse 17
Verse 16	Verse 18
	Verse 19
	Verse 20 I will create/do this miracle.

"Since the phrase 'do not be afraid' is repeated so often in this section of the book, we know it is a central issue for the people in captivity. They are afraid God has abandoned them, so Isaiah reminds them again and again that this will not happen."[9]

"The word 'Redeemer' appears here in 41:14 for the first time in Isaiah, but it will appear thirteen more times between now and the end of the book."[10]

As you reflect on these verses, how would you summarize the possibilities for those who choose to accept God's offer of help?

Instead of being weak like a worm that can be crushed by others (v. 14), Israel will become a strong instrument that can crush mountains and conquer its enemies (v. 15).[11] After talking about worms, soil, crops, mountains, and water, Isaiah then returned to legal imagery as he encouraged God's people to think clearly about God and idols.

CONSIDER THE EVIDENCE

READ ISAIAH 41:21-29. Summarize the evidence given against idols.

How does verse 24 define those who choose idols?

The Hebrew word in verse 24 used for "worthless" or "nothing" is *tow'ebah*, which means, "a disgusting thing, abomination, abominable."[12] Counterfeit comforts at best can't help, and at worst offend our gracious God. When we let anything capture our hearts and imaginations more than Him, idolatry can creep into our lives.[13] The Lord calls us to consider the evidence.

We all experience moments when we need a hand to hold. Perhaps we grieve a loss, fear the future, regret the past, or are just plain tired. In those times, we look for relief. Let's take a moment to evaluate where we turn for comfort.

Identify some godly sources of comfort you have turned to in the past or could turn to moving forward.

God reaches out His hand, so we want to identify and pursue practices that posture us to receive His help. Some godly comforts in my life include journaling, talking through problems with a friend, and sitting quietly with a hot cup of tea to reflect. Your list might look totally different. And remember, godly comforts don't have to be super spiritual. A hot bath, nap, or walk can relieve stress and help you rest in the Lord.

My daughter may have squeezed my hand through her injections, but over the course of her alopecia battle, I could never bring the relief she needed. Only the Lord got her through the dark days of being bullied, feeling ugly, and struggling with her identity. People and practices can help us in some moments, but only the Lord Himself can offer us the strength and help that brings lasting comfort. We need the Holy Spirit to help us consider the evidence as we ask ourselves whether we are reaching for fakes or the hand of the Real Deal—the God who tells us:

> For I hold you by your right hand—I, the LORD your God.
> And I say to you, "Don't be afraid. I am here to help you."
> ISAIAH 41:13

DAILY WRAP-UP

Today we focused on this truth: *God offers His hand of help, but we must turn away from counterfeits in order to receive His comfort.* **How would you summarize your personal takeaway from today's study?**

PRAYER

Lord, help me to trust my future into Your hands. You see all that is ahead for me. I want to reach for Your hand when life is scary rather than looking other places for comfort and strength. In Jesus's name, amen.

MEMORY VERSE ACTIVITY

Read Isaiah 40:31 aloud one time. Then write it down in your book or on a separate piece of paper.

Day Three

COMFORT IN CRISIS

SCRIPTURE FOCUS
Isaiah 43

BIG IDEA
God doesn't promise to remove all difficulties in our lives, but He does comfort us with His presence.

When I sat at my daughter's bedside in the hospital, I wondered if life would ever look the same. After going into septic shock, she could only breathe with the help of a ventilator, and our pediatrician warned us that she might not live through the night. I couldn't imagine life without our spunky five-year-old. I had so many questions and feelings, but in that room I felt God's presence thick in the air.

Throughout the next two weeks in the hospital she slowly recovered, coming off the ventilator only to battle a life-threatening blood clot. That was a season when smaller issues like arriving late to an appointment, locking my keys in the car, or feeling weary over long to-do lists paled in comparison to our current crisis. The seasons when trials are intense or long are described by Isaiah with metaphors like "deep waters," "rivers of difficulty," and "the fire of oppression" (Isa. 43:2). These aren't irritations; rather, these are times when it feels like the ground is shaking beneath our feet.

We jumped from Isaiah 41 to 43, but we will return to Isaiah 42 on Day Five to explore Jesus as our Source of comfort.

Before you dig into Isaiah 43, reflect on a time (or season) that felt like deep waters, rivers of difficulty, or fires of oppression in your life. Keep that season in mind as you read the words of comfort God delivered through Isaiah.

Today's verses in Isaiah comfort us as we remember that God doesn't remove all the difficulties in our lives, but He does comfort us with His presence.

COMFORT IN GOD'S PRESENCE

> You might be reading this in a public place, but if possible, I'd love for you to read Isaiah 43:1-13 out loud. Then summarize the first five verses in your own words.

I pray that reading these verses aloud connected with you and comforted you whether you are in the shallow or deep end with your own personal trials. God created, formed, and ransomed you. He calls you by name and promises to be with you because He is your God (vv. 1-2). He says you are precious and loved, so you shouldn't be afraid (vv. 4-5). No one can snatch you out of His hand (v. 13).

This week our focus is on trusting God's comfort. The Hebrew word translated into our English word for *comfort* is *nacham*. It means "to be sorry, console oneself, repent, regret, comfort, be comforted."[14]

> Which truth in the first part of Isaiah 43 is particularly comforting to you today, and why?

God directed these words to people who would become familiar with crisis when their cities would burn, and they would be relocated from their homeland to the foreign land of Babylon. The Lord wouldn't abandon them, but He would allow the discipline of exile. Their striving for idols and human comforts wouldn't deliver them. Eventually, their pain would give them vision to see their need for the Lord and His deliverance. Isaiah's message pointed them to the identity of the One who would save them. He would be present in their trials, and He will be present in ours.

We never want to forget that we can trust God's comfort even when our lives are turned upside down.

COMFORT IN GOD'S VICTORY

READ ISAIAH 43:14-28. What did the Lord promise to do for the exiles in Babylon (v. 14)?

What character qualities and displays of power in the past did God bring to their attention (vv. 15-17)?

What did the Lord tell them to do with the memories of the past, and why (vv. 18-19)?

What did the Lord say He would do with their sins (v. 25)?

These verses show us the priority of grace. The Lord didn't rescue His people because they were well-behaved. He comforted them because He is a faithful and forgiving God. That is good news for you and me because we also need rescue from our sin and struggles. A New Testament example of this same grace appears in Romans:

> But God showed his great love for us by sending
> Christ to die for us *while we were still sinners.*
> **ROMANS 5:8, EMPHASIS MINE**

The Lord also instructed His people to forget the past because He was doing a new thing. One commentator pointed out that God's fundamental principles don't change but His methods flex with changing needs: "We are meant to reflect on the past with gratitude and stimulated faith but not to stereotype our expectations from God."[15] Isaiah's language was reminiscent of the exodus when Moses led the people out of captivity (Isa. 43:15-16). Last time God delivered through the waters of the Red Sea, and this time He would make a way through the desert.

Our God wants to do new things in our lives too! His principles don't change—His Word never fades, but His present deliverance might take a different shape than His rescue in the past. We can't expect the Lord to work according to a past formula because He is a God who does new things.

As you look back on your journey of faith, what are some constants that have never changed?

Isaiah helps us glimpse God's gift of Himself and our responsibility to respond to His invitation. As we experience God's comfort, we can share it with others.

COMFORT TO SHARE

Read the following verse and circle the word *comfort(s)* each time you find it:

> He comforts us in all our troubles so that we can comfort others. When they are troubled, we will be able to give them the same comfort God has given us.
> 2 CORINTHIANS 1:4

What are some tangible ways people have comforted you?

When people are going through "deep waters," "rivers of difficulty," or "the fire of oppression" (Isa. 43:2), we want to be sensitive in what we say and do. Since my husband is a pastor, we've walked alongside people who've lost loved ones to suicide, parents who've learned of a cancerous brain tumor in their young child, spouses who've learned of an affair, and a variety of other tragic circumstances. In these difficult times, we want to avoid Christian clichés and learn from the model of God's comfort.

In Isaiah 43, we discovered God's comforting words:

- "I will be with you" in difficult times (v. 2).
- You are "precious," "honored," and "I love you" (v. 4).
- I "will blot out your sins" and "never think of them again" (v. 25).

These are words of comfort we can share with others in their pain. When my daughter was in the hospital, a man in our church wrote us a letter that I could barely finish for the tears welling up in my eyes. He attended our church, but I didn't know him personally. He had heard the updates regarding our daughter during a church service, and he felt nudged by the Holy Spirit to take a day off work so that he could fast and pray for my daughter's recovery. Knowing that someone was going before God's throne in prayer alongside us on behalf of my daughter strengthened our faith and comforted our family. In addition, meals from our small group, cards from fellow kindergarten students, and gifts of books and games to pass the time in the hospital supported our family in practical ways.

> Take a moment to think of someone you know who is going through deep waters. Write his or her name below and consider how you might comfort that person in a practical way.

PRAYER

Lord, You know what I'm walking through right now. Comfort me so that I can comfort others for Your honor and glory. Help me to know what to say and what not to say. Thank You for loving me, forgiving me, and assuring me that I won't drown in this river of difficulty! In Jesus's name, amen.

MEMORY VERSE ACTIVITY

Write down Isaiah 40:31. Also record one thought you have as you read over this verse.

The Lord helps us through our difficulties with His love and presence, but He also calls us to share His comfort with others. The Israelites didn't ask for God's help, and they grew tired of Him. God called them to repent, but He didn't abandon them. Instead, He told them to forget the past and get ready for new things ahead. No matter what the past week, month, or year has held for us, we can start afresh today by receiving God's comfort and helping others do the same. Whether you are coming out of a trial, in the midst of the fire, or headed into the flames, hold onto the truth that the Lord loves you and is nearer than you think.

DAILY WRAP-UP

> Today we focused on this truth: *God doesn't promise to remove all difficulties in our lives, but He does comfort us with His presence.* How would you summarize your personal takeaway from today's study?

Day Four

COMFORT IN RETURNING TO GOD

Before we jump into today's study, let's take a moment to review what we've covered so far this week to help us trust in God's comfort rather than strive to soothe ourselves when life is hard. We've found:

- God's promise to comfort the weary (Isa. 40).
- God's offer of His right hand of help (Isa. 41).
- God's comfort during seasons of crisis (Isa. 43).

  As you reflect on the first three days of study you completed this week, what truths stand out most in your mind regarding God's comfort?

SCRIPTURE FOCUS

Isaiah 44

BIG IDEA

God invites us to come back to Him when we've gotten off course.

Today's chapter in Isaiah adds an important element in our arsenal of truths regarding God's comfort. We can trust Him because He never stops calling us to come back to Him.

YOU BELONG TO GOD

> **READ ISAIAH 44:1-5.** Record some hopeful truths that stand out to you.

One of the first things I noticed in these verses is that God tells His people not to fear (v. 2). This command, given so often in Scripture, reassures us that the Lord knows our tendency toward anxiety. He reminds us often that we don't have to be afraid because we can trust Him.

The mention of God's Spirit also leapt off the page. God poured out His Spirit on all believers in the book of Acts and continues to indwell followers of Jesus with His Holy Spirit today. Isaiah had already mentioned the Spirit in 32:15, but again he gives this glimpse that the Spirit's work is to enable God's people to do what they cannot do on their own.

While these reassurances of God's help were great reminders, what hit me the most was verse 5. Though the Lord was speaking directly to the descendants of Israel, He also spoke of future generations of people who would take the name of Israel as their own by writing God's name on their hands (Isa. 44:5). For Isaiah's early audience, this description would have brought to mind images of a servant being marked on the hand with the sign of their master.[16] Think about how the New Testament writer Paul often referred to himself as a servant of God in order to honor the Lord's authority as Master in his life (Rom. 1:1; Phil. 1:1; Titus 1:1).

Reading this made me want to take out a marker and write "Yahweh" on my hand to mark myself as belonging to God! If we identify God as Master in our lives, we have marked our hands with His name spiritually, no Sharpie® required. We are some of the descendants God had in mind in verse 3. It blows my mind that God was thinking about us here in the pages of Isaiah. Whether we are of Jewish or Gentile descent, God invites us into a personal relationship with Him! Being marked as a servant means we belong to Him.

The New Testament expands on this concept of belonging even more by showing us that through Jesus we move from God's servant to God's heir.

READ GALATIANS 4:4-7 BELOW. Underline the benefits we receive as those who belong to God.

> But when the right time came, God sent his Son, born of a woman, subject to the law. God sent him to buy freedom for us who were slaves to the law, so that he could adopt us as his very own children. And because we are his children, God has sent the Spirit of his Son into our hearts, prompting us to call out, "Abba, Father." Now you are no longer a slave but God's own child. And since you are his child, God has made you his heir.

We are more than just servants. Through Christ we are children who receive a spiritual inheritance of eternal life. Our sin can guilt us into feeling like we aren't the sons and daughters of God, or don't deserve to be. But the same God who spoke these words to idol-worshiping, forgetful Israel is the God who speaks them to us today. These truths

from Isaiah 44 and Galatians 4 bring us comfort and hope when we don't feel like we belong anywhere.

Based on these verses, how does God respond to repentant sinners who humbly come back to Him?

How have you personally experienced God's grace when you have returned to Him on the other side of a wandering season?

Whether we've gotten off course for a short or long period of time, the Lord welcomes us back into relationship when we return. He comforts us with the promise of restoration but also warns us of the consequences of counterfeits.

THE FUTILITY OF COUNTERFEIT GODS

READ ISAIAH 44:6-20. **Summarize in a few statements why God says idols are foolish.**

> "The language Isaiah uses rests on the border line between poetry and prose, so that it cannot be put firmly into either genre. This is not however uncommon in the prophets."[17]

The Lord says the idol-maker never stops to reflect that he is literally making his own god (v. 19).

> He trusts something that can't help him at all. Yet he cannot bring himself to ask, "Is this idol that I'm holding in my hand a lie?"
> ISAIAH 44:20b

Without deeper reflection, we can fall into the same trap. One of the ways the Lord calls us to come back to Him is by reminding us to think deeply about the counterfeits we hold in our hands.

We may not carve our idols out of wood, but when we turn to comforts that provide short-term release and long-term regret, God calls us to reflect. What we have in our hearts ultimately ends up in our hands. Is the thing we are holding in our hands, thinking about in our minds, watching with our eyes, or shoving in our mouths really going to satisfy? This is a question we might need to ask more regularly. We must consider whether our creature comforts can actually deliver. God invites us to return to Him even if the last five times we turned toward counterfeits. We are never past the point of coming back to Him again.

THE CALL TO RETURN

The Hebrew word for *return* is *shuwb* and two definitions for this word used more than nine hundred times in the Old Testament include "to return, turn back" and "to reverse, revoke."[18]

> **READ ISAIAH 44:21-28.** Write verse 22 below, putting the word "RETURN" in all caps.

We find comfort in God's call to come back to Him again and again. It is possible for us to return to Him because of His faithfulness to redeem us rather than our good behavior. The Hebrew word in verse 22 is *ga'al*. This is the same word used of a kinsman redeemer in Jewish culture, a close relative who could restore property and honor to those who had lost it (Ruth 2:20). *Ga'al* means "to redeem, act as kinsman-redeemer, avenge, revenge, ransom."[19] We can return to God because He has chosen to pay the price for our sins through a promised Messiah.

> **What actions did Isaiah suggest based on the Lord's redemption (v. 23)?**

We've seen the Lord consistently plead His case against idolatry throughout this week. Here is a brief look at the progression we've seen:

- Idols aren't able to explain the meaning of the past or tell the future (41:21-29).

- Idols aren't able to save their people or keep the Lord from saving them (43:8-13).

- Idols aren't able to predict the future or save their worshipers from it (44:7-8).

Singing and shouting celebrated the good news that we don't have to stay on the wrong path. We can return to God as many times as we need to because He has paid the price for our sins.

What would it look like for you to answer God's invitation to return to Him in your present season?

We want to move toward God, but we don't always know what first steps to take. Here are some ideas to consider after wandering down the path of wrong thoughts, attitudes, or actions:

- Choose to reconnect with a friend who builds you up spiritually and speaks biblical truth into your life.
- Memorize Scriptures that especially speak to your current struggles.
- Remove apps from your phone that hinder or distract you from wholehearted devotion to God.
- Write prayer requests on slips of paper and put them in a mason jar. Pray over a few each day.
- Go for a prayer walk outside while confessing sin and asking God for direction.

These are just a few ideas to help get your creative juices flowing. They are not a prescriptive checklist to approach with a striving posture. Coming back to the Lord might mean you stop doing something that is not good for you, or it might mean pressing into practices like praying, studying God's Word, or attending church. Returning is ultimately about a change of direction in your mind and will.

In modern Christian circles, we often talk about turning our hearts toward God. The Hebrew understanding of the heart wasn't about feelings. Instead, the heart referred to the mind and the will. Think about it as putting your spiritual car in reverse if you have been driving away from the Lord with your choices and deciding instead to head toward Him with both your mind and your will. He is waiting for you.

He calls us back . . .

- Even when we've messed up again and again;
- Even when we repeat the same mistake;
- Even when we've said we're "sorry and want to change" a hundred times before.

MEMORY VERSE ACTIVITY

Attempt to write out Isaiah 40:31 from memory. Then check to see how you did.

God never considers us too far gone. In His grace He offers us freedom from our sin patterns and empowers us to pursue holiness, but we will never stop sinning completely this side of heaven. That means we must make a habit of coming back to God again and again for forgiveness and comfort.

In our study of Isaiah's message, we have read the words of a prophet committed to God. But his response in God's presence was, "It's all over! I am doomed," and he referred to himself as a man of unclean lips (Isa. 6:5). Isaiah messed up just like you and I do. Even as God's prophetic mouthpiece, Isaiah knew he didn't always say and do the right things. The Lord continued to use him despite his imperfections.

The many Messianic references in Isaiah point to the future sacrifice of Jesus as the pathway to redemption, the way we return to our holy God in the midst of our struggle with sin. Whether our sin falls into the category of small mistakes or major mess-ups, we have a Redeemer who has paid the price to set us free. He made us and will not forget us. Just as the Lord continued to work in Isaiah's life, He is always working in us too—conforming us more and more to the image of His Son.

DAILY WRAP-UP

Today we focused on this truth: *God invites us to come back to Him when we've gotten off course.* **How would you summarize your personal takeaway from today's study?**

Day Five

COMFORT IN CHRIST

My grandmother made me feel seen as a child. I can still envision her huge grin when any of her grandkids arrived at her home. When she was in her nineties, I took three days off my typical work schedule to fly to Texas to spend time with her. We walked down memory lane during those days, and she shared stories I had never heard about growing up during the Great Depression. I was able to tell her again how her love impacted my life. The next year we had to cancel our family trip to Texas because of the COVID-19 pandemic. Without any family coming to see her, she began to decline rapidly and ended up passing from this life to the next only a few months into the lockdown. I know she is with Jesus now, but oh how I miss her.

We couldn't gather as a family at that time to celebrate her life, and grieving in isolation was challenging. I wanted to be with others who knew the same pain I was experiencing. While none of our grief looks exactly like another's, we can find comfort alongside those who have similar circumstances. When someone can say, "I know this kind of pain," it normalizes our suffering so we don't feel totally alone.

> **Can you think of a season of suffering in your life when you found comfort from those who had walked a similar path?**

While we can certainly find support from others, today we will discover One who can truly comfort each one of us. No matter the source of our suffering, Jesus came to strengthen and support us. He set us free in a way no one else could because His suffering accomplished a restored relationship with our Creator. He would bring light and liberty to the world according to Isaiah's revelation of the Suffering Servant.

SCRIPTURE FOCUS
Isaiah 42

BIG IDEA
Christ offers comfort as the Servant who understands suffering.

We find four passages in Isaiah referring to God's Messiah with poetic language often referred to as the Servant Songs.[20] The term "Servant Songs" is a little misleading as there is no evidence they were ever sung.[21]

CHRIST'S SUFFERING

We've encountered "servant" language in other places in Isaiah that often referred to the nation of Israel as God's servant. In those passages the servant is personified as fearful and blind although loved by the Lord. God used this servant to evidence Himself to the nations. In contrast, the Servant Songs (Isa. 42:1-4; 49:1-6; 50:4-11; and 52:13–53:12) reveal a Messiah who is always obedient to God and whose mission is to bring light and justice to the nations.[22] This Servant would bring hope and comfort.

> **READ ISAIAH 42:1-9.** Record what stands out to you about the Lord's chosen servant.

Perhaps you noticed:

- He is the chosen One who pleases the Lord (v. 1).
- God put His "Spirit upon Him" (v. 1).
- He "will bring justice to the nations" (v. 1).
- He "will not crush" those who feel broken or burnt out (v. 3).
- He was called to demonstrate righteousness (v. 6).
- He will open blind eyes and free captives (v. 7).
- The Lord told His people the future before it would happen. Remember these words were written approximately seven hundred years before Christ's birth.

> Thinking about what you know of Jesus from the New Testament, how do you see Him as the fulfillment of this Messianic prophecy?

We may all have different answers, but some things I considered include:

- How the Holy Spirit descended on Jesus when He was baptized (Matt. 3:16);
- How Jesus approached a woman broken in sin. He didn't crush her but called her to repent (John 8:1-11);
- How Jesus healed a blind man (John 9:1-7);
- How I was a slave to sin, and Jesus set me free with the power to obey Him.

Now let's turn to a New Testament passage that puts to rest any doubt that these prophecies in Isaiah 42 refer to Jesus.

READ MATTHEW 12:15-21. Note what Jesus was doing just before Isaiah's words were quoted.

Jesus was healing the sick. He had compassion for those who were suffering. He understands that we are a people who often feel like a bruised reed or a candle on the verge of burnout. We can find others to console us when we experience brokenness and weariness, but only Jesus can ultimately bring the kind of healing we need. Jesus understands our pain personally. We can find comfort in His love and realize that following Him sometimes means following a path of suffering.

Unger's Bible Dictionary defines the "bruised reed" in Isaiah 42:3 as those who are: "spiritually miserable and helpless."[23]

SUFFERING WITH CHRIST

Read the verses below and underline the words *suffer* or *suffering* as you encounter them:

And since we are his children, we are his heirs. In fact, together with Christ we are heirs of God's glory. But if we are to share his glory, we must also share his suffering.
ROMANS 8:17

I want to know Christ and experience the mighty power that raised him from the dead. I want to suffer with him, sharing in his death.
PHILIPPIANS 3:10

Instead, be very glad—for these trials make you partners with Christ in his suffering, so that you will have the wonderful joy of seeing his glory when it is revealed to all the world.
1 PETER 4:13

Since our Messiah was prophesied to be a Suffering Servant, I wonder why I'm always relatively shocked at the sting of suffering in my own life. My son recently updated his prayer requests with our family in an app we use on our phones to pray for one another. He wrote several requests but the last one read,

"Pray that I would process through these questions:
1. What does it look like for me to suffer for Christ in my life?
2. Where am I running away from suffering for Christ?
3. How can I actively love others by putting their needs first in my life?"

He added a note that he doesn't want suffering for suffering's sake. Instead, he wants to adjust his view to align with biblical suffering. I share his requests with you not to brag about my kid. I have plenty of stories of my children's failures and sins that would knock me right off any parenting pedestal. I share this because I believe a realignment to a biblical view of suffering is needed in my life and maybe in yours as well.

Take a moment to apply my son's three prayer questions to your life. In the space below or on a separate piece of paper, jot down any ideas or thoughts next to each question from above.

Jesus knows you will suffer—sometimes because you live on a broken planet, other times as a result of your own poor choices, and perhaps even because you are a Christ-follower. In the midst of it, you can hold onto these truths: Jesus understands pain. Jesus won't crush you in times of brokenness. Jesus came to bring you freedom through His suffering.

We can trust in God's comfort because He sent Jesus as His Servant on our behalf. Our suffering doesn't mean the Lord doesn't love us. Instead of striving to avoid suffering, we can stir our affections for Jesus. He can use the good and the bad in our lives to draw us nearer to Him. For the people in Isaiah's day, the Lord told them way ahead of time that He would send a Servant to save them. We are privileged to know His name is Jesus and benefit from the progressive revelation that gives us a more developed picture of God's Servant.

READ PHILIPPIANS 2:6-8. God elevated Jesus to the place of highest honor after He fulfilled His humble service. How is the Lord calling you to take the attitude of Christ in the midst of your current challenges?

In the second part of Isaiah 42, we find a song of praise (vv. 10-17). One scholar pointed out that if we see the unity of this chapter, it would be natural to see the chief cause of praise as the work of the Servant we just read about.[24]

To end today, either write your own words of praise to the Lord or write Isaiah 42:12 as your personal heart-cry.

Finding others who share our struggles can be helpful, but it is good to know that we all have access to Jesus. You can sing even on dark days because Jesus is the Servant of the Lord who will not crush you; He will free you! He fulfilled the words of Isaiah as the Messianic Servant who comforts the broken. Through the tears I shed when I lost my grandmother, I sensed His nearness. His name is the hope of the nations and our personal hope when we feel bruised and burnt out. Let this truth sink deep and bring you comfort today.

DAILY WRAP-UP

Today we focused on this truth: *Christ offers comfort as the Servant who understands suffering.* How would you summarize your personal takeaway from today's study?

PRAYER

Lord, thank You for sending Jesus, a tender and loving Servant. Thank You for bringing light and liberty to my life. Give me a biblical view of suffering so that I don't have a skewed view of You when I'm feeling broken and on the verge of burnout. You are my hope when life is dark and difficult. Help me to see You clearly in those times and worship You in the midst of grief. I want to trust Your comfort today. In Jesus's name, amen.

MEMORY VERSE ACTIVITY

Write down or say aloud Isaiah 40:31 from memory.

Session Four
VIDEO VIEWER GUIDE

To access the video teaching sessions, use the instructions in the back of your Bible study book.

Where we look for comfort will either _____ or _____ us spiritually.

Not all pleasures are profitable for _____ (1 Cor. 10:23).

We can't be idle about _____.

Your _____ will shrink to the level of the _____ you pursue.

Idols give us association with _____ without a _____ to the Comforter.

We want the truth that will build our _____ so that we will trade these counterfeits in for the Comforter.

• He will renew our _____ (Isa. 40:27-31).

• He will not crush you when you feel _____ (Isa. 42:1-4,8).

• He will be with _____ (Isa. 43:1-5).

WOW: _____

_____

WOE: _____

_____

ACTION STEP: Point and _____.

Session Four
GROUP DISCUSSION GUIDE

SHARE: What is your go-to comfort activity?

WATCH the video "Session Four: Trust God's Comfort" (27:34 minutes) together and follow along with the viewer guide on the previous page.

MEMORY VERSE
Review Isaiah 40:31 and give the group an opportunity to recite it aloud.

VIDEO DISCUSSION
1. *Ask:* What circumstances have you longing for comfort?
2. *Discuss:* What are some practical ways that you seek comfort from the Lord?

STUDY DISCUSSION
1. Call on someone to read Isaiah 40:1-2; 40:31 aloud. Ask women to share how they answered this question from Day One (p. 73): *As you consider your own weary seasons, how have you experienced God's comfort through tender words or shepherding care?*
2. Review the headings for Isaiah 41 in Day Two: *Consider the Judge, Consider His Offer, Consider the Possibilities, Consider the Evidence.* Then ask women to share how they answered the Daily Wrap-up question found on page 81.
3. Select a woman to read Isaiah 43:1-13 aloud. Discuss which truths in these verses hit home with any current circumstances group members are going through.
4. Ask women to share how they answered this question from Day Four: *How have you personally experienced God's grace when you have returned to Him on the other side of a wandering season?* (p. 89)
5. Encourage someone to read Isaiah 42:1-3 out loud. Discuss what stood out from these verses and how they can bring comfort in difficult seasons.

REVIEW
Review the Big Idea for each of the five days of study. Ask for final thoughts or questions regarding the study of God's comfort from Isaiah this week.

PRAYER REQUESTS
Find a simple hourglass timer (or something similar perhaps from a board game). Allow women to share their key prayer request before the sand runs out. This helps women gather their thoughts and leaves more time for actual prayer rather than extended sharing of prayer requests.

TRUST *God's* COMMANDS

SESSION FIVE

Trusting God's commands in a world that tells us to follow our feelings can be challenging. He longs to give us the peace that comes with doing things His way, but we wander off His path continually. This week we will look at several truths from Isaiah that help us understand why God's commands matter and the consequences of failing to obey them. The amazing truth is that God knows we can't obey Him perfectly because of our sin natures, so He promised to send a Messiah to save us. Right living is possible only through Jesus's incredible sacrifice. Let's sit at Isaiah's feet this week and listen for the Holy Spirit to address any areas where we can grow in trusting God's commands.

MEMORY VERSE

Who among you fears the LORD
and obeys his servant?
If you are walking in darkness,
without a ray of light,
trust in the LORD
and rely on your God.

ISAIAH 50:10

Day One

COMMANDS THAT LEAD TO PEACE

BIG IDEA
God calls us to listen and obey His commands that lead to peace.

I was in a Bible study once with a woman who shared honestly about her struggle with passages in Scripture that contain God's commands and correction. She grew up in a home where good behavior and church attendance gave their family a public reputation that didn't match the abuse behind closed doors. She admitted that her childhood trauma often clouds her lens when reading Scripture. A counselor helps her separate her earthly father's behavior from her heavenly Father's.

As we begin our next two weeks of study in Isaiah with a focus on trusting God's commands and correction, we want to be sure we hold onto God's character and heart behind His instructions and identify places where, like my friend admitted, our own filter of experience might skew our understanding. This is something we all struggle with, whether we realize it or not.

> Take a moment to consider your own scriptural lens. How might other authorities or experiences in your life (past or present) impact the way you approach God's commands in the Bible?

Here is what we must remember: God's instructions are not tainted by a human sin nature. You may not have endured spiritual abuse, but your parents, church leaders, employers, teachers, and other authorities have all been imperfect. At times, they may have punished you unfairly, or their own lives may not have reflected the standards they enforced on others. When it comes to the Lord, though, we want to be careful not to transfer the behavior of imperfect human authorities onto Him. In Isaiah's message, we will find that His commands invite us closer rather than push us further from Him. Today we will discover that listening to God's commands leads to peace. I know peace sounds really good to me right now, and I hope the thought of peace appeals to you as well.

OUR DISOBEDIENCE PROBLEM

Last week when we left God's people, Isaiah's message predicted their exile in Babylon. Isaiah 48 reveals prophetic messages regarding their return back to their homeland from their captivity.

READ ISAIAH 48:1-11. What is the first command given in this chapter (v. 1)?

How did the Lord describe the people living in exile (vv. 4,8)?

Why did the Lord say He would hold back His anger (vv. 9,11)?

These verses aren't the feel-good ones we find on T-shirts or coffee cups. They remind us that God takes stubbornness and disobedience seriously. As we think about trusting God's commands, we have to consider the nature of rebellion. Throughout Isaiah and all of the Bible, we find this truth:

Humans suffer a chronic problem with disobedience.

In many passages of Scripture, we read about people with a habit of turning away from their Maker. One scholar said it this strongly, "From beginning (1:2) to end (66:24) the book of Isaiah is addressing rebellion."[1] I wish I couldn't so readily identify with my own tendency toward self-sufficiency. Depending on the Lord isn't my natural default, and I'm guessing it isn't yours either. Our sin nature doesn't direct us toward obedience. All of us struggle to stay within the boundaries God provides. This problem started in the garden of Eden when Adam and Eve ate from the tree God marked as "off limits" and continues to plague each one of us.

Rebellion can be defined as the refusal to "stay within the lines. Rebellion is not an ignorant missing of God's ways. It is an intentional and deliberate refusal to do what we know we should, and beneath that is the rejection of a relationship of dependence that acknowledges God has the right to declare what is right and wrong for us."[2]

Isaiah used words like "stubborn" and "obstinate" as well as summaries of those who were stiff-necked and hard-headed (v. 4). While none of us want to use these types of words to describe ourselves, we have to admit that the struggle hits close to home.

Complete this simple exercise acknowledging just one area where you recognize your struggle to obey a command that is clear in Scripture. Fill in the blanks:

__Tanya__ [your name] often struggles with God's command to _have a relationship daily_ . (Pick any one you like.)

In order to grow in trusting God's commands, we must acknowledge our propensity to ignore them. We need the Lord's help—His Word, His Spirit, His community—to support us in our pursuit of obedience. We can't comply on our own. And even when we get off course, the Lord doesn't turn away. Instead, He disciplines us like a loving Father and charts a course back to Him. In Isaiah 48 we see His plan to do this with Israel by bringing them back to Jerusalem after their time of discipline had ended.

LISTEN AND OBEY

God doesn't delight in correction, so He encourages us to listen to His commands. This is our second key truth from Isaiah 48:

God calls His people to listen and obey.

The very first word of chapter 48 includes the command to "hear" or "listen." In Hebrew this word is *shama. Shama* doesn't just mean to understand facts; it also carries with it the implication of obedience to what is heard.[3] A call to *shama* begins the chapter, but the same word is found a total of ten times in chapter 48.[4] When God repeats a word that many times in one chapter, we want to take notice!

READ ISAIAH 48:12-22. Fill in the chart below in your own words. (I did three of them for you.)

WHAT WE LEARN ABOUT GOD	WHAT HE COMMANDS US TO DO	WHAT HE WANTS FOR US
Verse 12	Verse 12	Verse 17
Verse 13	Verse 14	Verse 18
Verse 16 He predicted the future. He is Sovereign and His Spirit gives messages.	Verse 16	Verse 19 Descendants not destruction
Verse 17	Verse 20 Be free, sing and shout.	Verse 20

As you look at the commands in the second column, what do you notice about God's desire for His relationship with His people?

I loved that God calls us to come together and come close. His desire is for depth of relationship. That can only happen as He reveals Himself to us. Through this revelation, we can worship and obey Him with understanding. We can trust His commands because they reveal the way God created people to live. So how can we *shama*—hear, listen, and obey—with greater intentionality so we can come closer to the Lord?

Take a few moments now to sit quietly before the Lord. Ask Him to reveal any areas in your life that need attention as you think about your choices and His commands. Then jot down any areas where you want to follow the Lord more closely.

We learned in our first week of study that God is holy which means set apart. We know that He calls us to pursue holy living because Scripture repeats it often. This command is found several times in Leviticus (Lev. 11:45; 19:2; 20:7; 20:26; 21:8) and is repeated in 1 Peter 1:16: "For the Scriptures say, 'You must be holy because I am holy.'" While God gives us grace in our failures, He also empowers us through His Spirit to live holy lives. Thankfully, we don't have to walk down the path of sin because God offers us "everything we need for living a godly life" (2 Pet. 1:3).

BLESSINGS ACCOMPANY OBEDIENCE

We won't ever be perfect this side of heaven, but we can grow in obedience to God's commands. And when we listen, God showers us with blessings. God is always faithful, but His blessings are sometimes contingent upon obedience. Now don't hear me saying you'll have health, wealth, and prosperity if you obey God.

> **Look back at Isaiah 48:18,22. Record the blessing God wants to give to the righteous but withholds from the wicked.**

The blessings God offers those who listen aren't circumstantial ease or material blessings. God's commands lead to life and freedom, and one of the side effects on this path is peace. God said He wanted to give His people "peace flowing like a gentle river" (v. 18) if they had only listened. We can't listen to and obey God to manipulate Him into granting us peace. Rather, we recognize that trusting God's commands with our obedience leads to a life of peace. In contrast, taking a stubborn, obstinate, stiff-necked, hard-headed posture toward the boundaries revealed in the Bible won't bring us peace.

Some of the most miserable times in my life have included seasons when I've been actively walking in sin. Those seasons are devoid of peace. All the worldly pursuits that promise peace don't deliver in the end. God said it clearly through the prophet Isaiah: "there is no peace for the wicked" (v. 22).

On a scale of 1 to 10, where is your peace level right now? I'm not asking about peaceful or chaotic circumstances. I mean how is the stillness in your soul?

1   2   3   4   5   6   7   8   9   10

No peace   Lots of peace

How might striving less and trusting God more contribute to more peace this week?

The Lord commanded His people to leave captivity in Babylon. At this point in history, there was no evidence for anyone in exile ever returning to their homeland.[5] God's people needed to trust God's command to do something that would seem impossible in their estimation. Isaiah referenced the exodus to remind them that they serve a God who can get water out of rock (v. 21). If He can do that, He can handle a return from Babylon. He can also empower you to obey Him. God offers supernatural power to help us, but He also calls us to active trust that evidences itself in behavior.

DAILY WRAP-UP

Today we focused on this truth: *God calls us to listen and obey His commands that lead to peace.* How would you summarize your personal takeaway from today's study?

MEMORY VERSE ACTIVITY

Read Isaiah 50:10 aloud three times. You can find it printed on page 101.

Day Two

INSPIRED TO OBEY

SCRIPTURE FOCUS

Isaiah 50

BIG IDEA

The contrast between the sins of God's people and the obedience of God's Servant inspires us to pursue obedience.

I knew something was off. I couldn't state any particular sin or wrongdoing, but I didn't feel good about the growing exclusivity among my friends. I remember a day at the local pool when one of them threw a towel onto the chair next to me as a woman who had visited our church entered the pool. My friend said, "I hope she doesn't think she can sit with us every day." My jaw nearly dropped. I also noticed conversations crossing the line into gossip more and more frequently. After months of neglecting to address these issues directly, a huge blow-up occurred with these same friends and ended over a decade of relationships. My choices to participate in gossip didn't bring consequences right away. However, pain eventually reached both the gossipers and their verbal victims. I found myself in both categories and mourned over my decisions and the painful losses associated with them.

Isaiah's message reveals that even when we don't immediately experience painful effects, sin is serious. The nation of Israel rebelled by chasing other gods over the course of many years. They likely thought they were getting away with it, but Isaiah warned that they would experience discipline first-hand through an exile in Babylon. Today's chapter alerts us to their skewed view of the cause of their suffering.

SIN AND SUFFERING

READ ISAIAH 50:1-3. What did the Lord say was the cause of His people's suffering?

Two different words were used to describe the true reason for the people's suffering in verse 1. The first is the Hebrew word *awon,* which one scholar defined as "inner perversion of the heart." The second is *pesha*: "willful rebellion."[6] Bible translators have used a variety of English words in an attempt to capture the Hebrew meanings:

- "Wrongdoings . . . wrongful acts" (NASB);
- "Sins . . . sins" (NLT);
- "Sins . . . transgressions" (NIV);
- "Iniquities . . . transgressions" (CSB, ESV).

These words hit close to home for us. After studying this passage yesterday, I found myself tempted to compromise one of my own personal values. I was having that internal dialogue justifying why it would be OK to make a small concession when the Holy Spirit brought to my mind the seriousness of sin in today's passage. When I focused on the truth that even little compromises affect my own soul and invite divine discipline, the decision to say "no" to sin was a little bit easier. That is my prayer for us today—that revisiting the suffering associated with sin will deter us from habitually practicing it.

> Write out a brief prayer asking the Lord to help you pursue right living and turn away from sin in your life.

While sin's connection with suffering can be a deterrent in our lives, its threat isn't enough to keep us away from it. We need divine assistance in order to obey God's commands.

IMITATING THE SERVANT

Right after Isaiah spoke about iniquities and transgressions causing pain, He recorded another Servant Song. Remember there are four poems in Isaiah foretelling the Messiah as a Servant. After the Lord reaffirmed sin as the cause of His people's exile, we find a poem to remind us that God's Servant Jesus is the ultimate answer to our sin situation.

READ ISAIAH 50:4-11. Write what the "Sovereign LORD" (NLT, NIV) or "Lord GOD" (CSB, ESV, NASB) did for the Servant (Jesus) in the following verses:

Verse 4:

Verse 5:

Verse 7:

Verse 9:

Sin is serious, but these verses remind us that striving against sin won't free us from its entanglement. Christ, the Servant, delivers God's people from sin. God knows we can't overcome sin without His help. He is on our side in the battle against sin! Four times in this passage the Servant used the name *Adonai Yahweh*—"Sovereign LORD" (NLT, NIV) or "Lord GOD" (CSB, ESV, NASB). By using the name *Adonai* (Master, My Lord) and *Yahweh* (the personal name for God) together, we see an emphasis on God's role as a master to be obeyed who also longs to have a personal relationship with us. I want us to see the New Testament connections with Isaiah 50:6 firsthand.

Read the following verses and underline any sections that relate to Isaiah's mention of the Messiah being beaten, mocked, or spat upon:

Then they began to spit in Jesus' face and
beat him with their fists. And some slapped him.
MATTHEW 26:67

And they spit on him and grabbed the
stick and struck him on the head with it.
MATTHEW 27:30

And they struck him on the head with a reed stick,
spit on him, and dropped to their knees in mock worship.
MARK 15:19

The guards in charge of Jesus began mocking and beating him.
They blindfolded him and said, "Prophesy to us! Who hit you
that time?" And they hurled all sorts of terrible insults at him.
LUKE 22:63-65

The Servant obeyed the Lord fully but still suffered, and we know that His pain didn't end with beating, mockery, and spitting. He died a criminal's death on the cross. Jesus said that if we want to follow Him, then we must deny ourselves and take up our own cross (Matt. 16:24). He isn't asking us to literally die, but to choose to die to our own desires, our own sins, so that we can live for Him.

If we believe this, our faith can't be a hobby or side-gig. It takes over our entire lives—our words, attitudes, and actions are shaped by God's Word on every subject. We stop trusting our own definitions or expectations of what is right and wrong and submit to His. When we follow the Servant, we are inspired to emulate Him.

RELIANCE ON GOD

Our memory verse this week is Isaiah 50:10. Write it below.

Isaiah used two different words to emphasize what those who fear the Lord and want to obey His Servant must do—*trust* and *rely*. The Hebrew word for "trust" is *batach*, which means "to trust in, to have confidence, be confident, to be bold, to be secure."[7] To "rely" is *sha'an* and means "to lean on, trust in, support."[8] In order to find light in our darkness, we can lean into the Lord and put our confidence in Him as our place of safety.

These two words line up well with our overall theme in Isaiah of striving less and trusting God more. Right on the heels of the call to trust and rely on God comes a strong warning against living in our own light and warming ourselves by our own fires. God's response to our self-reliance has the same consequences as sin. Making idols out of people, work, material goods, self-sufficiency, or anything but the Lord will ultimately bring suffering.

In what area of your life is the Lord calling you away from striving in human effort and toward reliance on Him?

We can trust God's commands, which means leaning into God's Word rather than our own understanding. The contrast between the sins of the people and the obedience of God's Servant inspires us to avoid sin and pursue obedience. This means we stop ignoring the Bible and submit ourselves fully to God's commands. In a world full of blurred lines, the Lord calls us to humbly trust Him and His righteousness. We can do this when we make His Servant, Jesus, our safe place and press into Him with confidence.

DAILY WRAP-UP

Today we focused on this truth: *The contrast between the sins of God's people and the obedience of God's Servant inspires us to pursue obedience.* **How would you summarize your personal takeaway from today's study?**

PRAYER

Lord, thank You for reminding me of sin's serious consequences. I want to turn from sin and turn toward You. Thank You for sending Jesus to rescue me from sin. I want to trust You more. Help me to rely on You by pressing into our relationship with my face set like stone, totally focused on loving You. Give me the discernment to see Your heart behind Your instructions. In Jesus's name, amen.

MEMORY VERSE ACTIVITY

Read Isaiah 50:10 aloud one time. Then write it down in your book or on a separate piece of paper.

Day Three
THE DISTINCTION OF LIPS AND HEARTS

Three of my children were college students when the COVID-19 pandemic relegated classes to move online. As they navigated virtual lectures coupled with less real-life interaction and structure, all of them struggled. One of them confessed to me as the months wore on that school started to feel more like a game than an education. If you knew the rules, you could get decent grades without really learning the content.

The lack of personal connection made this a situation ripe for external compliance without internal transformation. They could go through the motions of school, pass the class, but not really have accomplished the goal of learning. This disconnect between original intent and actual accomplishment can also become blurred in our spiritual lives.

Israel built a temple, made sacrifices, and gathered for worship with the initial goal of authentic relationship with their personal God. They understood His holiness, His requirements, and His mercy through atonement. Their animal sacrifices were designed by God to foreshadow the ultimate sacrifice—Jesus dying to restore intimacy between a sinful people and a holy God. Over time, though, many of their spiritual practices drifted from heartfelt expressions to religious checklists. They began to trust in the observance of their faith rather than the object of it.

We can find ourselves in this same struggle. We may have started reading our Bibles, praying, going to church, or serving in ministry out of love for the Lord. But over time a drift can happen when we lose sight of our "why." God calls His people to shift their heads and hearts back into alignment. Israel's rebellion was an outward symptom of the deeper issue of wayward hearts. The words of Isaiah we will examine today reveal to us that trusting God's commands goes beyond external compliance (giving Him lip service) to internal transformation (letting Him change our hearts).

SCRIPTURE FOCUS
Isaiah 29; 30

BIG IDEA
Trusting God's commands isn't just about external compliance but internal transformation.

THE PROBLEM WITH HYPOCRISY

Chapters 28–35 in Isaiah are sometimes labeled the "woe" oracles because of the repetition of the Hebrew word *hoy* ("woe"), warning of actions that displease the Lord.[9] Much of God's displeasure is related to His people's idolatry and hypocrisy.

READ ISAIAH 29:1-4,13-16. Describe God's indictment in your own words.

Referring to Jerusalem as "Ariel" is found only in Isaiah 29. "One possible meaning of the word is 'altar hearth.'"[10] This would fit with the complaint against Jerusalem's external altar sacrifices that lacked genuine worship.

From these verses, it seems as though Jerusalem claimed immunity from God's judgment based on their sacrifices and worship. The Lord made clear He was not pleased with worship and obedience that didn't come from the heart. Like my college kids who learned how to work the system without actually learning the content, we must guard against going through the motions of worship when our hearts and daily actions are far from God. God doesn't want empty or hypocritical ceremonies whether in Isaiah's day or ours. He gave rituals to reinforce—not replace—spiritual truth.

As you think about your acts of worship and obedience, where does it feel like you're going through the motions spiritually?

How often are you expecting encounters with God in your private and corporate worship?

During His earthly ministry, Jesus encountered people who needed to hear Isaiah's words about heartfelt worship. Some Pharisees (major rule-followers) criticized Jesus for not mandating that His disciples perform traditional handwashing procedures. Jesus quoted Isaiah in correcting their logic.

READ MATTHEW 15:7-9. Circle the words *hearts* and *lips* when you read them:

> You hypocrites! Isaiah was right when he prophesied about you,
> for he wrote, "These people honor me with their lips,
> but their hearts are far from me. Their worship is a farce,
> for they teach man-made ideas as commands from God."

The Pharisees were known for putting heavy weights on people by heaping on extra rules. As we study God's commands this week, we aren't looking to compound any guilt we already experience in our struggles. Instead, any guilt is removed when we learn to trust God and obey Him from the heart.

In Isaiah 29, we find alternating messages of judgment and hope. We've read the judgment passages, so now let's explore God's mercy.

WORSHIP FROM THE HEART

Judgment is very much a part of Isaiah's message, but it is not the final word. Hope is the final word. God calls His people to know Him, trust Him, and love Him. When they choose to walk in rebellion, He disciplines them to help them realize what they are missing—real relationship with their Creator. His temporary judgment can lead to permanent hope when His people trade religious routines for personal intimacy with God.

READ ISAIAH 29:5-8,17-24. Write down two or three hopeful things the future holds for God's people.

Look again at verse 23. Rather than checklists or personal pride, what is the motivation for genuine worship?

Trusting God's commands isn't about white-knuckle obedience and behavior modification, it's about allowing God to transform us from the inside out as we fall more in love with Him. Our God is the Holy One, and we are His creation. We were created for the sole purpose of glorifying Him. As we understand who He is and who we are in Christ, we can worship from the heart.

READ ISAIAH 30:15,18-22 and summarize God's message in verse 15 in your own words.

What are some specific ways you can trust God more in your acts of worship and obedience—prayer, Bible study, church attendance, ministry activity, and so on? List as many as you can think of.

In order for me to return, rest, ask, and wait for the Lord, I've realized I must create margin for these types of activities in the midst of a busy life: reflecting, taking quiet walks, praying, journaling, active listening, reading God's Word, intentionally releasing worries, and limiting technology. We try so hard to figure out next steps in our human striving when Scripture documents the Lord speaking most often in the quiet. He promises to teach us and guide us. Isaiah 30:21 says when we ask for help and then wait patiently for Him, we will hear a voice telling us, "'This is the way you should go,' whether to the right or to the left." When we shift our focus off of ourselves and toward God, we show Him that we believe He is enough and we trust Him with our details.

Pick one of the realignment ideas from the list you just made. Write it below, and put when and where you will make space for it in your planner or calendar. Use that as an opportunity to trust God more.

PRAYER

Lord, I want to worship You with my mouth and my heart. Change me from the inside out. My behavior needs to change, but help me to trust Your commands in returning, reflecting, and in quiet pursuit of You! In Jesus's name, amen.

Today's popular messages encourage us to just believe in ourselves. They tell us to do what we want, believe what we want, and live how we want. The resounding call of "you do you" parallels the postures that brought judgment for the nation of Judah. Instead, we want to trust God's commands so we don't place our confidence in the wrong places, like empty religious motions and our ability to save ourselves. By pursuing intimacy with Him, we can stay connected to His heart behind the commands. We don't want to engage in worthless worship, so we seek God's help to align our lips and hearts.

DAILY WRAP-UP

Today we focused on this truth: *Trusting God's commands isn't just about external compliance but internal transformation.* **How would you summarize your personal takeaway from today's study?**

MEMORY VERSE ACTIVITY

Write down Isaiah 50:10. Also record one thought you have as you read over this verse.

Day Four

INSTRUCTIONS PRECEDE CONSEQUENCES

SCRIPTURE FOCUS
Isaiah 58; 59

BIG IDEA
God clearly communicates His commands so we will understand His expectations.

When our kids were young, they often played in the basement of our home. Sometimes, they emerged upstairs for me to referee fights. Although we had clear family rules, they would justify themselves and make excuses when they got in trouble, like claiming they didn't know they weren't supposed to throw things or hurt their sibling while wrestling. We eventually posted a piece of construction paper on the wall for clarity with a list of rules like: No hitting. No throwing. No wrestling. No yelling. No biting. The kids could no longer say they weren't aware of the rules when they broke them because the warnings were clear.

The Lord may not use a piece of construction paper, but He has clearly communicated His standards. As we seek to trust God's commands, we want to lean into the importance of seeking His heart behind His instructions. Remember it was the Pharisees who followed the letter of the law but missed God's intent. Let's read today's passages curiously knowing that the Lord gave these warnings about sin so that His people would know what pleases Him and what doesn't.

BLESSINGS FOR OBEDIENCE

READ ISAIAH 58. Circle the letters that best answer the following questions:

What displeased the Lord regarding the people's fasting (vv. 3-4)?

A. They did it to please themselves.
B. They continued oppressing their workers while fasting.
C. They kept on fighting and quarreling.
D. All of the above.

What other commands did the Lord give His people (vv. 9-10)?

A. Stop spreading rumors.
B. Remove the heavy yoke of oppression.
C. Feed the hungry and help those in trouble.
D. All of the above.

What commandment did God instruct the people to observe carefully (vv. 13-14)?

A. Work harder.
B. Honor the Sabbath.
C. Judge others.
D. All of the above.

As you consider these commands given through Isaiah the prophet, which ones are still important for Christians to obey today?

The commands given through Isaiah are important for believers today, they just look different in practice. When it comes to keeping the Sabbath, we don't have the same rigidity of observance as the Jewish people. Jesus didn't cancel God's call to rest, but He did fulfill the law and become our place of spiritual rest (Matt. 12). Fasting is still an important spiritual discipline, as long as people fast with a humble heart to draw near to the Lord, not to please themselves and "feel" spiritual. Trusting God's commands means knowing them and asking for His help to understand how to live them out today.

What are some practical ways Christians live out God's commands?

• Sharing food, shelter, and clothing with those in need (Isa. 58:7,10):

• Refraining from gossip and spreading rumors (v. 9):

• Prioritizing rest as a regular spiritual practice (v. 13):

As you consider how you can grow personally, which one of these commands needs attention?

Prioritizing rest stood out to me. When my children were smaller, we observed "media-free" Sundays. We took naps and walks, played games, and made this day different from others with no laptops or phones. (They all hated it at the time but reflect back on it with gratitude!) However, since they have all moved out, I find myself failing to take time to engage in restorative activities with the same kind of intention.

Before we move on to chapter 59, I don't want us to miss the blessings the Lord wants to bestow on those who trust His commands. We read in Isaiah 58 that those who obey the Lord would experience:

- Salvation coming like the dawn (v. 8);
- Wounds quickly healing (v. 8);
- Godliness leading them forward (v. 8);
- God's glory protecting them from behind (v. 8);
- The Lord answering their call saying, "Yes, I am here" (v. 9);
- Their light shining out from the darkness (v. 10);
- The Lord guiding them continually and restoring their strength (v. 11);
- Flourishing like a well-watered garden (v. 11);
- Returning to their homeland as a rebuilder and restorer (v. 12);
- The Lord honoring them and satisfying them with His promised inheritance (v. 14).

What stands out to you as you read through this list of blessings?

Not only does the Lord warn us about His expectations before bringing consequences, He also gives us an opportunity to turn back to Him and receive incredible blessings. As I reflected on these blessings, I noticed that godliness would lead us forward and God's glory would protect us from behind. The Lord hems us in from both sides as a shield. I also couldn't help but observe the reference to the rebuilding of walls that

Isaiah prophesied more than a hundred years before the exile and the return of men like Ezra and Nehemiah who would help reestablish the city of Jerusalem. God knew the future, and He gave His commands well in advance—written on scrolls—so His people could refer back to them. You and I are some of those people who read them today and can learn to trust God's commands!

CONSEQUENCES FOR DISOBEDIENCE

READ ISAIAH 59:1-8. Summarize in your own words God's message about sin:

Isaiah said sin starts in people's minds and then gives birth to action (v. 4). The world loves to disguise sin as shiny and fun, but the Lord says that it leads to danger and bondage. Isaiah used the metaphors of "deadly snakes" and "spiders' webs" to illustrate this principle. He also said that the people had "mapped out crooked roads, and no one who follows them knows a moment's peace" (Isa. 59:8). The road to sin doesn't lead to peace but instead to suffering and entrapment.

READ ISAIAH 59:9-21. What illustrations were used to describe sinners in verses 9-11?

What things did Isaiah say were gone according to verses 14-15?

What did the Lord do since no one helped the oppressed (vv. 16-17)?

Who would the Redeemer come to save (v. 20)?

The apostle Paul quoted Isaiah 59:8 in Romans 3:10-18 when talking about the wages of sin and Christ's sacrifice.

Several times in today's passages we encountered the themes of light and darkness. Isaiah reminds us that aligning our lives with God's truth will lead us to light in a dark world. Running on the path toward sin will only take us further into the darkness.

What would the Lord give that would never leave them (v. 21)?

Look at the good news Isaiah delivered! The Lord would step in and redeem His people by sending a Redeemer, who we know to be His Son, Jesus. This Redeemer would restore sinful people back to Him. He would also give His Spirit and His Word to sanctify them in their daily battle with sin.

We can't claim ignorance regarding God's commands or excuse ourselves by stating our confusion over which rules to obey. That is the stuff of kids and basements! It reveals our immaturity rather than our desire to strive less and trust God more. Instead, we want to press into God's truth, discern His directions, and embrace the blessings and peace that obedience brings.

DAILY WRAP-UP

Today we focused on this truth: *God clearly communicates His commands so we will understand His expectations.* **How would you summarize your personal takeaway from today's study?**

MEMORY VERSE ACTIVITY

Attempt to write out Isaiah 50:10 from memory, then check to see how you did.

Day Five

RIGHTEOUSNESS IN CHRIST

Sometimes when we study God's commands, we can feel overwhelmed by how easy it is to get off track. Though we might desire to fully obey the Lord, we lack the ability to follow through in all areas. This can leave us discouraged as we think about our position before a holy God. Thankfully, our God knows we can't become righteous by our own efforts. Although today's chapters contain some weighty truths, they also encourage us as we read about God's plan to free us from the penalty of sin. My prayer as you study today is that Isaiah's prophecies about Christ, the Suffering Servant, would encourage you and confirm your faith.

THE CALL TO LISTEN

READ ISAIAH 52:1-12. Describe in your own words what Isaiah says to God's people regarding:

- Preparing to leave captivity (v. 1): *Clothe yourself in your strength and in beautiful garments*
- His name (v. 6): *people shall know MY NAME "Here I am"*
- The messenger He will send (v. 7):

- The manner in which they will leave (v. 12):

This chapter began with the words, "Awake, awake" (NASB, NIV), or "Wake up, wake up" (CSB, NLT). Remember, when we see a word repeated (like "Holy, holy, holy" in 6:3), we want to pay attention. The Hebrew word translated "awake" is *uwr* and means, "to rouse oneself, awake, awaken, incite."[12] Isaiah is rousing us from the reverie of human effort and calling us to pay attention. Let's awaken today as we focus on the greatest message of all time—the truth that God sent His Son, Jesus, to die in our place so that we could be made righteous through His sacrifice.

SCRIPTURE FOCUS
Isaiah 52; 53

BIG IDEA
Jesus bore the consequences for our disobedience.

Isaiah 52 and 53 foretell Jesus's sacrifice through a fourth and final Servant Song with such clarity that skeptics can't explain the parallels except to say that Jesus must have intentionally modeled the details so people would know He was the Messiah.[13]

THE SERVANT'S SACRIFICE

After awakening his audience and predicting freedom from Babylonian captivity for God's people, Isaiah transitioned to the prophetic Servant's sacrifice that brings freedom for all people for all time.

READ ISAIAH 52:13–53:12. Using the chart that follows, briefly describe the Servant according to each verse. Next, make a note of any parallels to Jesus using the New Testament references I've given you in the last column. I did the first one for you.

ISAIAH PASSAGE	DESCRIPTION OF THE SERVANT	PARALLEL TO JESUS	NEW TESTAMENT REFERENCE
52:14-15	His face was disfigured so he hardly seemed human. He will startle many nations. Those who have never been told about him will see and understand.	Paul quoted these verses in Romans to describe Christ. The crown of thorns and beatings disfigured Jesus as Isaiah described.	Matthew 27:28-30; Romans 15:21
53:1			John 12:37-41; Romans 10:16-17
53:2-3			Matthew 27:22-25; John 1:46; John 12:37-43; John 15:20-21; John 19:1-3
53:4-6			Matthew 8:14-17; 1 Peter 2:19-25

ISAIAH PASSAGE	DESCRIPTION OF THE SERVANT	PARALLEL TO JESUS	NEW TESTAMENT REFERENCE
53:7-8			Luke 23:8-9,24-26; Acts 8:32-35
53:9			Matthew 27:57-60; Philippians 2:8; 1 Peter 2:19-25;
53:12			Luke 22:36-38; Luke 23:34

What stood out most to you in these verses?

The description of Jesus as hardly recognizable as a human made me recall the depth of pain He endured. When I think that Jesus did this so the punishment for my sin could be transferred to Him, I feel the weight of it. I'm also captivated by the metaphor of sheep going astray. All people wander away from God's path like sheep. So God sent Jesus to be the "Lamb of God who takes away the sin of the world" (John 1:29). He gave Himself up for us as the perfect sacrifice to pay for our sins, sacrificing Himself on behalf of the flock.

Though the original readers of Isaiah's words didn't have all the details, they learned that their righteousness would be found through a Servant sent on their behalf. Isaiah made it clear that ultimate victory over sin would come not through triumphant conquest but through an obedient Servant enduring rejection and abuse. It's important for us to understand that Jesus willingly endured what we read about in Isaiah's prophecy. When one of Jesus's disciples wanted to fight against the officers who came to make an arrest, Jesus said to him,

> Put your sword back into its sheath. Shall I not drink
> from the cup of suffering the Father has given me?
> JOHN 18:11

Earlier that night, Jesus hinted at what was to come for Him. During the last supper with His disciples, He foretold His substitutionary death:

> And he took a cup of wine and gave thanks to God for it. He gave it to
> them and said, "Each of you drink from it, for this is my blood, which
> confirms the covenant between God and his people. It is poured out as
> a sacrifice to forgive the sins of many. Mark my words—I will not drink
> wine again until the day I drink it new with you in my Father's Kingdom."
> MATTHEW 26:27-29

Jesus prepared His disciples as best He could. He also prayed for strength to endure the suffering He knew was coming while in the garden of Gethsemane. Colossians helps us feel the weight of what Christ's suffering accomplished for us:

> For God in all his fullness was pleased to live in Christ, and through him
> God reconciled everything to himself. He made peace with everything
> in heaven and on earth by means of Christ's blood on the cross.
> COLOSSIANS 1:19-20

How would you summarize in your own words what Christ's sacrificial death accomplished?

Our response to Isaiah 53 is to decide personally whether to accept or reject Jesus's sacrifice. Either write from memory or look up John 3:16 and write it here:

Each one of us must choose to believe and receive God's free gift. He said He would send a Messiah to save us, and He did.

> **Take a moment to reflect on your response to Christ's sacrifice on your behalf. If you're a Christian, describe below how and when you believed in God's love, sin's separation, and Christ's payment for sin to restore your relationship with God. If you haven't accepted Christ's sacrifice personally, what is holding you back from making this decision today?**

PRAYER

Father, thank You that Your Son endured suffering and rejection on my behalf. I couldn't meet my greatest need, so You provided the way for my reconciliation to You. Awaken me often to these truths so I don't become apathetic to what You have done for me. You are my righteousness! Help me to strive less and trust You more. In Jesus's name, amen.

Every person will one day stand before God. The difference between eternal life with God or eternal separation from God will be what we believe about His Son. Passages like Isaiah 53 remind us that God went to great lengths to save us. It was a high price, but Jesus paid it for us. As we reflect on the Servant in Isaiah 53, we find He didn't come just to tell us God's commands. He came in part to live in obedience to them for us. He came to exchange His life for ours. Righteousness comes not from doing our best but from putting our faith in Christ. Isaiah calls us to wake up to these truths. Like sheep, we often leave God's paths to follow our own. We can't produce our own righteousness in our human strength. Only through trusting in Christ's sacrifice can we be made right with the holy God.

DAILY WRAP-UP

> **Today we focused on this truth:** *Jesus bore the consequences for our disobedience.* **How would you summarize your personal takeaway from today's study?**

MEMORY VERSE ACTIVITY

Write down or say aloud Isaiah 50:10 from memory.

To access the video teaching sessions, use the instructions in the back of your Bible study book.

You can't __hide__ your __heart__, because what's in your __heart__ will show up in your __habits__.

Lips __lie__, but __lives__ don't (Isa. 29:13).

God doesn't see __worship__ apart from the __worshiper__.

God's reaction to people's rebellion is a call to __listen__ (Isa. 30:15,20-22).

We need to __rely__ on __God__ (Isa. 50:10).

We should trust His commands because they are for our __good__.

WOW: __J.C. died for me__

WOE: __J.C. died for me J.C. called us to come and die to ourselves ~~asking~~__

ACTION STEP: Ask God, "What are You __asking__ of me?"

Session Five
GROUP DISCUSSION GUIDE

SHARE: What plant, tree, or flower is your favorite?

WATCH the video "Session Five: Trust God's Commands" (27:29 minutes) together and follow along with the viewer guide on the previous page.

MEMORY VERSE
Review Isaiah 50:10 and give the group an opportunity to recite it aloud.

VIDEO DISCUSSION
1. *Ask:* Was Isaiah's message focused on behavior modification or internal transformation? Why is this distinction important?
2. *Discuss:* How is your listening life lately? What steps do you want to take to become a better listener to God and others?

STUDY DISCUSSION
1. Direct someone to read Isaiah 48:18 aloud. Ask women to share how they rated their current peace level on page 107. Then discuss the follow up question: *How might striving less and trusting God more contribute to more peace this week?*
2. Ask volunteers to share how they summarized their personal takeaways in the Daily Wrap-Up on page 112.
3. Select a woman to read Isaiah 30:15 and 30:18-22 aloud. Brainstorm together specific ways to trust God more in acts of worship and obedience. (They can refer to their answers to this question on p. 116).
4. Share some of the practical ways Christians can live out obedience in the areas listed in Day Four (on pp. 119-120). Then ask volunteers to share how they answered the question: *As you consider how you can grow personally, which one of these commands needs attention?*
5. Ask women to share what stood out to them from Isaiah 53.

REVIEW
Review the Big Idea for each of the five days of study. Ask for final thoughts or questions regarding the study of God's commands from Isaiah this week.

PRAYER REQUESTS
Make today's prayer time "popcorn prayer" style. Open a time for women to say a word or phrase of praise to God. Then transition to words or phrases regarding requests they have for the Lord. As the leader, close the prayer time with a few sentences to wrap up.

TRUST *God's* CORRECTION

SESSION SIX

Sometimes people get tripped up when they try to read through Isaiah and come to chapters 13–34. These verses include graphic descriptions of God's corrective measures toward many nations. Reading them from a modern mindset can challenge our view of a loving and forgiving God. This week we'll explore these passages with a desire to know God and understand His righteous anger. His mercy will overshadow judgment, and we will see His discipline as a loving act—for us as well as for the original hearers of Isaiah's message. Together we'll discover how to get back on the right path when we've strayed. The seriousness of pride and arrogance in these chapters will help us embrace the humility plan. We'll see that Jesus is not only a Suffering Servant but also a righteous King who has the authority to correct us. While the Scriptures we read this week may startle us at times, they are great reminders of the gravity of sin and the mercy of our God.

MEMORY VERSE

Lord, your discipline is good,
for it leads to life and health.
You restore my health
and allow me to live!

ISAIAH 38:16

Day One
HOPE AND JUDGMENT

BIG IDEA

We can trust the Lord's correction to help us get back on track when we veer toward sin.

One summer in college while on a mission trip in Japan, I got separated from my group and had to take a bus to meet my team. I walked out of a train station and saw no less than fifteen different buses. I thought I understood which one to board and sat listening intently for my stop to be called, but when the bus pulled back into the station, I was the lone passenger. To say I was feeling a little panicked at that point would be an understatement. The driver motioned for me to come into the building, found someone who spoke English, and made a phone call. Thankfully, a kind worker drove me to my team, which took almost an hour!

I was headed in the wrong direction, and I needed correction to get me back on the right path. As we read some passages this week that contain harsh language regarding God's judgment, we want to remember His intent. The Lord invites all people into relationship with Him, and one of His key character qualities is justice. He is fair in all He does. When the people He created treat each other unjustly, He often intervenes. The consequences may not always be on our timetable, but we can trust that God will right the wrongs in our world in His way and in His time. This week, we will focus our attention on what we can learn from examples of behaviors that consistently invited God's correction.

A GLIMPSE OF GOD'S CORRECTION

If you're reading the "Read Through Isaiah" plan (I hope you are! It's on page 184.), then you have already read Isaiah 13–34 and God's judgments against nations like Babylon, Assyria, Philistia, Moab, Egypt, Jerusalem, Judah, and even the whole earth. Phew! These chapters contain a lot of harsh words from our God. Since we can't comb through all these chapters together, I'll quickly cover some of the highlights.

One thing that stands out in these chapters is that God's words of judgment for specific individuals, cities, and nations were always preceded by sinful behaviors and patterns. Most commonly, those included pride, idol worship, oppression of others, self-sufficiency, and a lack of trust in God.

Why would these behaviors warrant the Lord's correction? What do they communicate to God about a person's belief in and relationship with Him?

List the opposite of each of these sins:

- Pride:

- Idolatry:

- Oppression of others:

- Self-sufficiency:

- Lack of trust in God: *surrender*

Why would behaviors and postures like the ones you just identified bring people into a closer relationship with God?

In Isaiah 24 and 34 we find indictments against everyone on earth with a general judgment for twisting God's instructions, breaking God's covenant, deceit, and rebellion.

As you consider behaviors that brought correction and the opposite postures that brought relationship with God, can you identify any areas in your life where you can pursue the Lord more fully?

The Bible is clear: God offers a relationship with Himself to the entire world. He chose to use His people as His mouthpiece with His message, but He desired to be close with people of all nations—and that has always been the case. Sprinkled throughout these chapters of Isaiah are tender words regarding how the Lord longed for everyone to repent of sin and draw near to Him. For example, God pursued the people of Egypt—the very ones who held Israel captive as slaves for more than four hundred years (Ex. 12:40-41).

Read the following verses and underline verbs that describe what God would do in Egypt:

> In that day five of Egypt's cities will follow the LORD of Heaven's Armies. They will even begin to speak Hebrew, the language of Canaan. One of these cities will be Heliopolis, the City of the Sun. . . . The LORD will make himself known to the Egyptians. Yes, they will know the LORD and will give their sacrifices and offerings to him. They will make a vow to the LORD and will keep it. The LORD will strike Egypt, and then he will bring healing. For the Egyptians will turn to the LORD, and he will listen to their pleas and heal them. In that day Egypt and Assyria will be connected by a highway. The Egyptians and Assyrians will move freely between their lands, and they will both worship God. In that day Israel will be the third, along with Egypt and Assyria, a blessing in the midst of the earth. For the LORD of Heaven's Armies will say, "Blessed be Egypt, my people. Blessed be Assyria, the land I have made. Blessed be Israel, my special possession!"
> ISAIAH 19:18,21-25

It's almost shocking for us to hear God refer to the nation of Egypt as "my people" (v. 25) considering their treatment of the Israelites, God's covenant people. But this is the perfect picture for us of the grace of the Lord. It's also important for us to understand that God didn't bring painful consequences to the Egyptians or the Israelites for no reason. His intention was healing (v. 22), to help them get off the road that leads to destruction and onto the path of intimacy with Him. Pain helped them see the futility of idols and human effort so they could identify their need for God. He disciplined with the hope of turning them back in the right direction.

Read the following verses and underline God's reason for the exile:

> Has the LORD struck Israel as he struck her enemies? Has he punished her as he punished them? No, but he exiled Israel to call her to account. She was exiled from her land as though blown away in a storm from the east.
> ISAIAH 27:7-8

Within these judgment chapters are sprinkled many verses regarding hope. God doesn't want to destroy His creation; He longs for them to be saved from damaging behaviors. When it comes to judgment and hope, Christians embrace these opposing truths simultaneously. Following the Lord means holding correction in one hand and hope in another. In faith, we hold both hands up in worship to God.

God's discipline isn't just an Old Testament concept. The writer of Hebrews in the New Testament said:

> For the LORD disciplines those he loves,
> and he punishes each one he accepts as his child.
> HEBREWS 12:6

Obeying God isn't easy, but enduring His discipline doesn't seem enjoyable either. We get to pick our "hard." When we consider our choice to trust God or strive in human strength, I hope we choose trust time and again.

Think back on a time when you have felt the balance of God's correction and hope in your own life. What is one word you would pick to describe that experience or season?

GOD'S HEART BEHIND HIS CORRECTION

READ ISAIAH 9:8–10:4. Then circle the words or phrases in the word bank below that angered the Lord. (Hint: There are eight to circle.)

PRIDE	HELPING THE NEEDY	TAKING ADVANTAGE OF ORPHANS	HYPOCRISY
ARROGANCE	WISE LEADERS	SPEAKING FOOLISHNESS	JUDGING FAIRLY
SEEKING GOD	FAILURE TO REPENT	INJUSTICE FOR THE POOR	WICKEDNESS

These verses highlight God's justice, one of His key attributes. Let's admit that this language about the Lord's judgment is graphic and hard to read. I don't have any great explanations for those of you who are struggling with this strong language, but what I know is that God is sovereign over everything, and He is serious about the right order of things.

Lord, I desire to follow You. Help me to remain humble, dependent, and mindful of Your truths. When I begin to stray, help me to get back on the path of faith quickly. Sometimes Your justice is difficult to understand through my lens. Help me to trust that You will ultimately make all things right. Please show me how I can be involved in helping the poor and oppressed! In Jesus's name, amen.

MEMORY VERSE ACTIVITY

Read Isaiah 38:16 aloud three times. You can find it printed on page 131.

The Hebrew word translated "justice" in Isaiah 10:2 is *mishpat.*[1] One scholar helps us understand its meaning when he says, "It is much more than merely legality, as 'justice' has come to connote in English. Rather, it has the idea of 'right order.'"[2] God's justice is also always in tandem with His compassion and patience, as we see many times throughout the Old Testament (Ex. 34:6; Num. 14:18; Neh. 9:17; Ps. 86:15, etc.).[3]

Because God is just, He determines the right order for things in the world as well as in our lives:

- He sets the boundaries for morality (Ex. 20:1-17; Ps. 51:4).
- He disciplines justly (Heb. 12:5-11).
- His posture toward sin is wrath (Ex. 34:6-7; Rom. 6:23).
- He cares about the treatment of the poor and oppressed (Ps. 82:3; Luke 11:42; Jas. 1:27).

God is just—He knows how things should be ordered in your life. When you believe Him by faith, you are inspired to act justly. I pray today's conversation inspires you to get things in the right order as you consider the behaviors and attitudes that either separate people from God or draw them closer to Him. God doesn't delight in correction, but He also doesn't want you to stay on the wrong path. He will do what He must to draw you back to Him. Although His judgments can seem painful in the moment, you can trust that His goal leads to a hopeful place of intimacy with Him.

DAILY WRAP-UP

Today we focused on this truth: *We can trust the Lord's correction to help us get back on track when we veer toward sin.* How would you summarize your personal takeaway from today's study?

STOP BEING REACTIVE

THE HUMILITY PLAN

I don't remember the destination of the drive, but I'll never forget the conversation I overheard taking place in the back of the van. One of my children complained about consequences she had received recently from my husband. She asked her older sibling why he never seemed to get in trouble. He said, "I know what makes dad angry and choose to avoid provoking him. It's not that I'm scared of dad or his punishment, but I obey out of love and respect." Upon reflection, my son's wisdom can also be applied to our interactions with God.

Yesterday we observed some behaviors exhibited by nations and individuals that angered the Lord and warranted His correction. One that stands out in Isaiah and throughout Scripture is pride. God consistently corrected those who trusted in their own strength. As we seek to strive less and trust God more, embracing humility will be a key posture for us. In order to trust, we must first admit our need for God.

The tension we sometimes encounter in a discussion about pride is that we mistake godly confidence for pride. Taking initiative or boldly using our spiritual gifts shouldn't be equated with pride. Pride says, "I got this!" Humility says, "God's got this!" Our ability to stay the course of submitting to God's will over our own is what I sometimes refer to as the "humility plan." This plan realigns us to see our mistakes, failures, and problems as reminders of how much we need the Lord.

Where have you been on the humility plan lately? What has reminded you of your need for God?

SCRIPTURE FOCUS
Isaiah 13–14

BIG IDEA
Pride repeatedly brings God's correction into the lives of people and nations.

"If anyone would like to acquire humility, I can, I think, tell him the first step," said author C. S. Lewis. "The first step is to realize that one is proud. And a biggish step, too. At least, nothing whatever can be done before it. If you think you are not conceited, it means you are very conceited indeed."[4]

Today our goal is to see how our God responds to pride and seek His supernatural help to identify it.

BABYLON'S EXAMPLE

READ ISAIAH 13. Describe Babylon's behavior that angered the Lord. (Pay close attention to v. 11.)

"The word *Babel* means 'gateway to a god' and sounds like the Hebrew word *balal*, which means 'confusion.' (Gen. 10:8-10; 11:1-9). In Scripture, Babylon symbolizes the world system man has built in defiance of God."[5]

Babylon was a nation known for its pride, and God corrected their sinful behavior. Like yesterday's texts though, we'll find that judgment and hope remain intertwined. The opening verses of chapter 14 begin with promising words regarding Jacob's descendants.

READ ISAIAH 14:1-3. Circle the numbers that correspond to the blessings found in these verses for Israel:

1. Have mercy on them.
2. Make them rich with material possessions.
3. Choose them as His special people.
4. Bring them back to settle in their own land.
5. Give them easy lives with no challenges.
6. Bring people from many nations to help them return and serve them in the land.
7. Allow them to rule over their enemies.
8. Give them rest from sorrow, fear, slavery, and chains.

While most scholars see the "king of Babylon" referenced in Isaiah 14 as a composite of all the proud kings who have ruled the earth, some have thought Sargon II of Assyria and his son Sennacherib may have provided models for the qualities written in the poem."[6]

What comes next in Isaiah 14:4-23 is considered by scholars to be one of the finest Hebrew poems in all of Scripture. It includes four stanzas that are written in the form of a lament or funeral song. Let's briefly examine each of these stanzas and see what they teach us about the sin of pride and the Lord's correction.

1. The Earth's Reaction to the King's Death

READ ISAIAH 14:4-8. Identify phrases that reveal the earth's reaction to the death of this Babylonian king.

Answers: 1, 3, 4, 6, 7, 8

The earth could sing again; it was at rest because the king of Babylon could no longer destroy it. Verse 8 specifically mentioned trees and woodcutters. Historically we find that "Assyrian and Babylonian monarchs were greedy for wood, and their woodcutters stripped whole districts of their trees."[7] Pride is a destructive force that impacts not only people but the ecology of the earth as well.

2. The Underworld's Response

> **READ ISAIAH 14:9-11.** Describe briefly the scene taking place in the underworld.

The place of the dead was referred to in Hebrew as *Sheol*. It was the equivalent of Hades in the New Testament (Luke 16:23). These verses don't inform our theology of the afterlife but provide a poetic mockery of human pride. What we learn here is that death is the great leveler. No matter how much you own, how much power you possess, or how great you look, "each person is destined to die" (Heb. 9:27). As we move into the next stanza, notice a shift in language. Prophets often began with local events and then expanded to grander principles.

3. Heaven's Perspective

> **READ ISAIAH 14:12-15.** Identify three of several "I will" statements that mark this prideful figure.

I will _____.

I will _____.

I will _____.

As you read these statements, what are your thoughts regarding whether these verses refer to a human king or to Satan?

No matter what conclusions we draw, we can all agree that pride and godliness can't coincide. Those who desire to become God's equal by elevating themselves actually distance themselves from the living God. Jesus stepped down from glory and took on the role of a servant. He embodied humility to the point of death (Phil. 2:5-8). Satan's pride pushed him out of relationship with God. In the same way, our independence and self-sufficiency create a barrier between us and God. Humility draws us back to Him.

4. A Reflection of Life on Earth

> **READ ISAIAH 14:16-23.** Describe the burial of this king in a sentence.

This great king's body was left out in the streets or thrown into an unknown burial pit, which would have been an act of ultimate humiliation. One commentator pointed out that Egyptian pyramids and other royal tombs reveal the importance of a proper burial—including ceremonial rites—in Old Testament times.[8] For the original readers of Isaiah's poem, this king's dire end would connect his pride with severe judgment.

EXAMINING OUR OWN LIVES

As we reflect on Isaiah 13 and 14 and the pride of Babylon, we want to make connections to our own struggle with pride. These chapters shouldn't dissuade us from having ambition or pursuing big goals, but they remind us to regularly check our motives.

> **What does our culture say makes a person great—either through overt messages or underlying worldviews embedded in our media, advertising, and entertainment? In contrast, what qualities does God value according to our study today?**

"The city of Babylon was completely destroyed in 689 BC by Sennacherib and the Assyrian army, but it was rebuilt by Sennacherib's son. In 539 BC, Darius the Mede captured the city, but he did not destroy it." After Alexander the Great conquered the city, it was never rebuilt—fulfilling Isaiah's prophecy.[9]

What we learn from Isaiah 14 is that greatness is not found in striving to ascend but in choosing to descend. This is the example Jesus set for us during His earthly ministry, and the way He teaches His followers to relate to others. For the Christian, the way up is down. Overcoming pride is challenging because ascending is in our nature.

> **Earlier today we recorded three "I will" statements spoken in the pursuit of pride. Ask the Lord to reveal any areas in your life where pride might be an issue. Then write your own "I will" statements but themed with humility rather than arrogance.**
>
> I will _____.
>
> I will _____.
>
> I will _____.

You could have written a variety of phrases to fill in those blanks including release control, make prayer a priority, or choose to think of others more highly than myself. Isaiah's teaching regarding Babylon reminds us that pride leads to death but surrender leads to life. Like a child who learns what angers his dad, we can know beyond a shadow of a doubt that pride falls into that category for our heavenly Father. Because we know that pride brings consequences, we can embrace the humility plan.

DAILY WRAP-UP

> **Today we focused on this truth: *Pride repeatedly brings God's correction into the lives of people and nations.* How would you summarize your personal takeaway from today's study?**

PRAYER

Lord, I want to humble myself before You. Pride comes naturally to me, but I know it doesn't honor You. Help me to learn from Isaiah's message that pride leads to death, but surrendering to Your will leads to life. Correct me right away when I take steps toward independent striving so that I can turn quickly toward trusting You more! In Jesus's name, amen.

MEMORY VERSE ACTIVITY

Read Isaiah 38:16 aloud one time. Then write it down in your book or on a separate piece of paper.

Day Three

TURN AROUND

SCRIPTURE FOCUS
Isaiah 17; 19; 20; 22; 27; 28

BIG IDEA
Repentance is the goal of God's correction.

When my children were little, disciplining them was one of my least favorite activities. I struggled because I dreaded the mental and emotional energy needed to do it consistently. It was easier to ignore bad behavior. My husband was much more consistent, but he struggled to stay calm when kids disobeyed or disrespected him.

Thankfully our God is a perfect parent. He doesn't have issues with being reactive or consistent. As we have already seen in Isaiah, God gives consequences in order to help people turn around when they are headed down the path of sin. This week's passages aren't the "feel good" Bible verses we find plastered on coffee cups or social media graphics. I'll admit that a part of me would like to avoid this week's chapters because they are full of harsh judgments. Reading about despair, destruction, and death brought by the Lord can be difficult to reconcile with the character of a loving and merciful God. But we know that "all Scripture is inspired by God" (2 Tim. 3:16), which means we need to lean into these chapters in order to see God's heart behind His correction.

GOD'S WAKE-UP CALL

Scholars have suggested that Christ's call for attention in the parable of the sower (Mark 4:3,9) reveals the influence of Isaiah 28:23-29, which also used farming metaphors and called the audience to listen.[11]

Our God loves us too much to leave us on the path of destruction without sending up signal flares to get our attention, and nothing wakes us up from the reverie of sin like pain. "Pain insists upon being attended to," said C. S. Lewis. "God whispers to us in our pleasures, speaks in our conscience, but shouts in our pains: it is his megaphone to rouse a deaf world."[10]

When something physically hurts in our bodies, it can mean an intervention is needed. A physician might need to set a bone, perform a surgery, or prescribe a medication. In the same way, our Great Physician may allow temporary discomfort in our lives for the greater good of long-term healing. God is willing to leverage our comfort to develop our character.

Let me be clear about one thing before you read any further: Not all pain in our lives comes from our own personal sin. Sometimes we are affected by others' sins or the general effects of living on a broken planet. Some pain isn't our fault, but other times we bring it on ourselves. Either way, God doesn't waste our pain. He will use it to develop our character and strengthen our relationship with Him.

Through Isaiah's message, the Lord revealed His purposes for the nations' pain. Read the passages in the left column and fill in the missing information in the chart.

PASSAGE	PEOPLE	PAIN	PURPOSE
Isaiah 17:4-11	Israel	Desolate fields, few people remaining, grief	Verses 7-8
Isaiah 19:1-10,18-25	Egypt	Fighting, confused plans, cruel masters, Nile dried up, despair, workers will be sick at heart	Verse 22
Isaiah 20:1-6	Egypt and Ethiopia	Verse 3	Verses 5-6 So nations would look to the Lord instead of other nations for help
Isaiah 22:1-14	Jerusalem	Verses 2-5	Verses 9-13 So people would learn to mourn and show remorse for sin; to teach people to seek help from the Lord instead of trusting human logistics
Isaiah 27:7-13	Israel (again)	Houses abandoned, streets overgrown with weeds, broken people	Verses 8-9

What stood out to you as you read these verses about pain and God's purposes?

While the consequences of sin may have seemed harsh at times, we learn that God doesn't punish His children; He corrects them. His motive is not to abuse but to realign His creation. We see God's gentle methods spelled out with the analogy of a farmer in Isaiah 28.

What did the Lord identify as Samaria's downfall (Isa. 28:1,3,7-8)?

What were the priests' and prophets' accusations against the Lord (28:9-10)?

What was the Lord's message to His people, and how did He communicate it (28:12-13)?

What do you think the Lord was trying to communicate regarding His corrective methods with the illustration of the farmer (28:23-29)?

In agriculture, a farmer uses different procedures at different times. His work involves plowing, sowing, threshing and grinding with the goal of producing a harvest. Isaiah's illustration reminds us that God's purposes require Him to act according to the need of the season. He also doesn't winnow every plant with the same method. Each crop is processed with the amount of pressure needed to produce the best end product. Like a farmer, the Lord will use the correct instrument to separate the worthless from the valuable in the harvest of our lives.

RESPONDING TO CORRECTION

Our pain can make us bitter against God, or it can lead us to turn toward Him.

READ 2 CORINTHIANS 7:10 BELOW. Then write your
own definitions for *godly sorrow* and *worldly sorrow* in the
spaces provided.

> For the kind of sorrow God wants us to experience leads us away from
> sin and results in salvation. There's no regret for that kind of sorrow.
> But worldly sorrow, which lacks repentance, results in spiritual death.
> 2 CORINTHIANS 7:10

- **Godly sorrow:**

- **Worldly sorrow:**

Godly sorrow turns us away from sin and toward God. *Worldly sorrow* refuses to turn
away from sin. Both are reactions we may have when we experience the Lord's correction
firsthand. When we understand God's correction is meant to help rather than harm,
we can recognize God's discipline as an expression of love.

Discipline takes intentionality, energy, and consistency. I remember my children
complaining often about consequences. My husband and I would tell them that we
disciplined them because we loved them. They would respond that if we loved them,
we wouldn't take away their phones or ground them from fun activities. I once showed
a particularly frustrated child Proverbs 13:24 in my Bible: "Those who spare the rod of
discipline hate their children. Those who love their children care enough to discipline
them." God cares about us enough to discipline us. He does it so that we might experience
godly sorrow over sin and turn toward Him.

How have you grown closer to the Lord through a difficult season? Think about specific painful circumstances and the lessons learned in hindsight.

PRAYER

Lord, You are the just Judge. Help me to trust Your correction in my life. When I feel sorrow over life's pains, help me to turn to You in the midst of them. Give me eyes to see Your heart behind discipline. Use pain as a megaphone in my life to help me focus on eternal rather than temporary things. In Jesus's name, amen.

MEMORY VERSE ACTIVITY

Write down Isaiah 38:16. Also record one thought you have as you read over this verse.

What is one decision you can make or action you can take to turn away from sin and toward God today?

God longs for us to stop striving in our human strength and instead trust Him more. He wants us to look to our Creator for help when we go through seasons of discipline. When we get off the path of obedience to Him, He calls us to account so that we can turn from sin and turn to Him. Today you may have sorrow, but know that it can be a godly sorrow that turns you around in a hopeful direction.

DAILY WRAP-UP

Today we focused on this truth: *Repentance is the goal of God's correction.* How would you summarize your personal takeaway from today's study?

Day Four

REVIVAL

Thoughts of a cup of tea often motivate me to get out of bed after hearing my alarm. I like holding a hot drink in my hands first thing every morning. I enjoy the taste but also the alertness that accompanies the caffeine rush. When it comes to a spiritual boost, we need more than a drink to revive us. Spiritual sluggishness affects all of us from time to time, and the Lord longs to bring revival into our lives. In Isaiah 57:15 we find the word *revive*, which in Hebrew means to "enliven" or "to cause life."[12] Sin brings death, but the Lord longs to give us life.

God's correction can feel heavy as we've experienced this week in the pages of Isaiah. Today again we will find God's anger stirred up by disloyalty and depravity. But anger doesn't have the final word. God's mercy triumphs over judgment (Jas. 2:13). His goal is to bring revival to our spirits and minds so that we experience abundant life.

BARRIERS TO REVIVAL

Isaiah 57 is written as a Hebrew poem that confronts the nation of Israel's movement away from God and toward idolatry. The poem follows a format of mercy (vv. 1-2), judgment (vv. 3-13), and then once again mercy (vv. 14-21).

> **READ ISAIAH 57:1-2.** Explain how God shows mercy to those who follow godly paths.

Even though the righteous died and it seemed like no one cared, God cared and promised to give them peaceful rest. Despite death, His hope and mercy are still realized, and the wicked will not have the last word.

SCRIPTURE FOCUS
Isaiah 57

BIG IDEA
Sin brings death, but the Lord longs to give us life.

A witch or sorceress in Isaiah's day referred to "one who has opened herself to control by a spirit or supernatural entity."[13]

In the next section of Isaiah 57, we want to identify key behaviors that angered the Lord. These sins deadened their responsiveness to God.

READ ISAIAH 57:3-13. Answer the following multiple-choice questions:

1. What questions did the Lord have for the idol worshipers (v. 11)?

   A. Are you afraid of these idols?
   B. Is that why you lied to Me and forgot My words?
   C. Do you no longer fear Me because of My long silence?
   D. All of the above

2. What did the Lord say He would do regarding what the people saw as "good deeds" (v. 12)?

   A. Reward them
   B. Applaud them
   C. Expose them
   D. Forget them

3. Who did God say would be rewarded by Him (v. 13)?

   A. Those who strive harder
   B. Those who worship idols
   C. Those who tolerate sin
   D. Those who trust in Him

God spoke through the prophet Isaiah to people who got way off track. The sins mentioned in Isaiah 57 were tied to idolatry, specifically to fertility cults that connected sexual worship with agricultural prosperity.[14] Instead of following Yahweh's prescribed worship, they worshiped gods like Molech who appealed to their sensuality and greed.

God exposes sin so people can see the futility of their choices. The people were determined and persistent but decidedly wrong. The objects of their affections were like smooth or slippery stones. Stones cannot speak, act, or move. They had "traded the truth about God for a lie" (Rom. 1:25). In the Lord's grace, He corrected them.

When we see the Israelites' behavior and God's strong reaction to it, we can exercise caution in our own lives. The apostle Paul wrote to his protégé Timothy about a people with parallel issues to those Isaiah described.

READ 2 TIMOTHY 4:3-4 BELOW. Underline the similarities between Isaiah 57:3-13 and these verses:

> For a time is coming when people will no longer listen to sound and wholesome teaching. They will follow their own desires and will look for teachers who will tell them whatever their itching ears want to hear. They will reject the truth and chase after myths.
> 2 TIMOTHY 4:3-4

How do you see the need for this warning in our current culture?

We want to be alert and revived so that we are careful in these ways:

- We listen to sound and wholesome teaching;
- We don't follow our own desires;
- We don't look for teachers who will tell us only what we want to hear;
- We embrace the truth and reject myths.

Isaiah 57 reveals that God gets angry when we believe myths that appeal to our earthly lusts. The people combined following God with compromising His clear commands. They sought after any god or religion that they believed would reward them with material blessings and physical pleasure. Today, the message of God's wrath toward sin is often downplayed in favor of emphasizing tolerance and self-expression. Itching ears would rather hear that we can practice behaviors that compromise God's truth *and at the same time* prop ourselves up with religious activities that make us feel spiritual. Isaiah's message assures us that we can't.

THE PATH TO REVIVAL

We can trust God's correction because He exposes sin to keep us from the consequences it brings. He also offers forgiveness and compassion to those who will turn from sin and turn to Him.

READ ISAIAH 57:14-21. What did the Lord say to "clear away" (v. 14)? Who did the Lord say He would "restore" and "revive" (v. 15)?

What did God promise to do—even for the greedy, stubborn people who made Him angry (vv. 18-19)?

What outcomes are given for those who continue to reject the Lord (vv. 20-21)?

I hope you noticed the "I will" statements the Lord made in today's verses. Earlier this week we read some "I will" prideful proclamations in Isaiah 14. Today, we find God telling us He will "heal," "lead," and "comfort" us (Isa. 57:18). Scripture tells us many times that our God is slow to anger and quick to compassion. One passage that especially parallels Isaiah 57 is found in Psalm 103.

READ THE VERSES BELOW and circle any words or phrases that highlight God's grace and mercy:

The LORD is compassionate and merciful,
slow to get angry and filled with unfailing love.
He will not constantly accuse us,
nor remain angry forever.
He does not punish us for all our sins;
he does not deal harshly with us, as we deserve.
For his unfailing love toward those who fear him
is as great as the height of the heavens above the earth.
He has removed our sins as far from us
as the east is from the west.
The LORD is like a father to his children,
tender and compassionate to those who fear him.
For he knows how weak we are;
he remembers we are only dust.
PSALM 103:8-14

In the original Hebrew of Isaiah 57:19 we find the word *shalom* twice. *Shalom* means, "completeness, soundness, welfare, peace."[15] God wants to give us the peace we so desperately desire, a peace that can only be found in Him. We won't find it in counterfeits or compromise. *Shalom* is at the heart of revival. The Lord longs to awaken us to more committed obedience to His ways because of His great love and compassion toward us.

I've been amazed over and over this week by the truth that the Lord loves me enough to correct me. He doesn't leave me on the path of sin without warnings and consequences to help me when I'm chasing the wrong things. Small compromises may not seem very serious in the moment, but today's chapter reminded me of the seriousness of sin. And as much as the Lord hates sin, He loves us so much more. I hope today you will hold onto the truth that He wants to heal you, lead you, and give you His peace!

> Take some time to reflect on how you can be more fully committed to following God's path in your Christian walk. Write out a prayer asking the Lord to revive your heart.

PRAYER

Lord, revive me. Put new life in me that I might follow You more closely. Help me to discern messages that lead me away from Your truth. Provide me with sound teaching rather than convenient messages that stroke my ego. Show me where I have compromised and lead me back to You. In Jesus's name, amen.

DAILY WRAP-UP

> Today we focused on this truth: *Sin brings death, but the Lord longs to give us life.* How would you summarize your personal takeaway from today's study?

MEMORY VERSE ACTIVITY

Attempt to write out Isaiah 38:16 from memory, then check to see how you did.

Day Five

ALREADY, NOT YET

SCRIPTURE FOCUS
Isaiah 11; 12

BIG IDEA
Jesus will return and bring perfect justice to all creation.

When my oldest child no longer needed a babysitter, my husband and I faced a dilemma. Our son was ready for independence, but his three little sisters still needed supervision, and they didn't want to have rules enforced or consequences given by their older brother. We came up with a plan to help keep the chaos to a minimum by having our son write down offenses rather than enforce rules. As parents, we would investigate and discipline as the ones who held authority over all of our children.

These initiatives were necessary because our son lacked the authority to correct the behaviors of his siblings. We aren't likely to trust the correction of someone we don't believe has the right to rule in our lives. I'm often skeptical of directives and authorities unless I believe they have a right to intervene in my life, or if I have willfully submitted myself to their leadership. I have no problem complying when I trust the rule-maker and rule-enforcer.

In our previous Day Five studies focused on the Messiah, we've seen Jesus depicted as our Suffering Servant. Today, we will see Him as a ruling authority. Jesus came to save, but when He returns a second time, it will be to rule. When we trust Him as our righteous Judge, we will be more open to His correction in our lives.

MESSIAH'S AUTHORITY

Isaiah employed the use of physical illustrations to reveal spiritual truths in Isaiah 11.

READ ISAIAH 11. Draw or briefly describe one of the images or metaphors you find:

You had several illustrations to choose from in these verses—a shoot coming up out of a stump, a belt or sash, predators and prey, or a highway. Let's look at each of these individually and see how they reveal Jesus as the Messiah with authority to rule in the lives of all creation.

1. A shoot from the stump of David (Isa. 11:1-2)

The stump with "new Branch" (11:1) represents the Messiah coming from the line of David. The dynasty of David hadn't existed for *hundreds of years* when Christ was born, so this stump served as a true metaphor for what would appear to be a dead kingdom. Christ is the righteous Branch that would come out of Israel, and the Spirit of the Lord would "rest on him" (v. 2).

Isaiah identified the stump with Jesse, who was King David's father. This reference to Jesse connects the Messiah with the line of David.

What are some of the words used in Isaiah 11:2-4 to describe the Messiah's rule?

Depending on your Bible translation you might have written words like *wisdom, understanding, power, knowledge, fear of the Lord, righteousness,* or *justice*. How do these qualities deepen your trust in Jesus's authority to direct and correct in your life?

The Lord will never get it wrong, so we can trust His correction. He doesn't judge according to outward appearances or hearsay. He has all the evidence, knows every motive, and is able to judge fairly.

2. A belt and sash (vv. 3-5)

The next metaphor we discover in Isaiah 11 is a belt and sash. Isaiah 11:5 says of the Messiah, "Righteousness will be his belt and faithfulness the sash around his waist" (NIV). A Hebrew sash was less like a waist ribbon and more like an "undergarment" (NLT).

As one commentator noted, "In the Near Eastern dress styles, the belt or sash (v. 5) was the garment that gave stability to the whole ensemble."[16] This image reveals that Christ was fully prepared for judgment with righteousness and truth as His foundation. His reign is held together by truth inside and out.

3. Predators and prey (vv. 6-9)

When Jesus returns in the future, He will fully restore peace to the earth. At that time, enmity between predators and prey will no longer exist. As we read this glimpse into the reign of the Messiah as King, we must acknowledge that although Jesus partially fulfilled these prophetic metaphors when He came to earth the first time, they have not fully come to pass on earth yet. The oppressed still seek justice, babies can't play near cobra's nests, and lions and lambs aren't lying down together.

We can't say exactly how these prophecies have been or will be fulfilled, but we can best understand them with the words *already* and *not yet*. Jesus has *already* fulfilled Isaiah 11 in that He came to earth as the righteous Branch. But elements of these verses have not yet been fulfilled. It makes me think about the glimpse we get of Jesus's eternal reign in Revelation 20–21. During the future reign of Christ, the earth will be free of aggression and chaos. This seems to be precisely what Isaiah described. Jesus has already come, but He will come again. The next time it will not be as the Servant in the songs we've studied in Isaiah. His next appearance will be characterized as a reigning King who restores all of creation.

4. The higher path (v. 16)

Isaiah closed this chapter with the image of a highway, one of Isaiah's favorite images.[17] The highway Isaiah had in mind isn't a literal road; it's a spiritual journey. Jesus is the Messiah who bridges the gap that sin created between the Father and His creation. Jesus's saving work has three key elements. In each one, we can clearly see the *already* and *not yet* at work in our individual relationships with Jesus.

- **Justification:** We become saved from the penalty of sin the moment we believe in our heart and confess with our mouth that Jesus is Lord (Rom. 10:9).

Some references to roads, paths, and highways in Isaiah:

- Isaiah 26:7-8
- Isaiah 35:8
- Isaiah 40:3-4
- Isaiah 42:16
- Isaiah 49:11
- Isaiah 57:14
- Isaiah 62:10

- **Sanctification:** We are being saved from the power of sin as God conforms us more and more to the image of His Son. This is an ongoing process that lasts our whole lives (Rom. 6–8).
- **Glorification:** We will be saved from the presence of sin when we are in heaven after our physical death or the return of Christ (1 Cor. 15).

Our salvation has happened, is happening, and will happen more fully when we trade this body for a new one! This leads us to praise the One who makes all this possible (2 Cor. 5).

READ ISAIAH 12 slowly as a prayer of praise to the Lord. Then write out the verse that most resonates with you.

We need not question our Messiah's authority. We can trust His correction because His will is to save us. I pray you will worship Him for what He has already done and live with expectant hope for the *not yet* that is still to come.

DAILY WRAP-UP

Today we focused on this truth: *Jesus will return and bring perfect justice to all creation.* How would you summarize your personal takeaway from today's study?

Session Six
VIDEO VIEWER GUIDE

To access the video teaching sessions, use the instructions in the back of your Bible study book.

We want to _____ the _____ of the _____.

We want to value _____ more than _____.

The Lord wants to turn us off the path to _____ and onto the path to _____.

Two sins God corrected:

    1. _____ (Isa. 26:4-6)

We don't want to exchange the plans of a _____ Father for the schemes of an _____ snake.

    2. _____ of the _____

God is more concerned about our _____ than He is our personal _____.

God's _____ _____ are perfect (Isa. 28:23-29).

There is no one wiser than _____ (Isa. 11:1-5).

WOW: _____

WOE: _____

ACTION STEP:

A _____

C _____

T _____

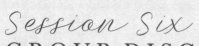

Session Six

GROUP DISCUSSION GUIDE

SHARE: What is your favorite way to travel, and why (plane, boat, train, etc.)?

WATCH the video "Session Six: Trust God's Correction" (29:43 minutes) together and follow along with the viewer guide on the previous page.

MEMORY VERSE

Review Isaiah 38:16 and give the group an opportunity to recite it aloud.

VIDEO DISCUSSION

1. *Ask:* How can the sins of pride and neglect of the poor in Isaiah's day be seen in our modern culture?
2. *Discuss:* What are some practical ways you can welcome God's warnings in your life?

STUDY DISCUSSION

1. Discuss together opposite words for the behaviors that invited God's correction found on page 133. Then ask women to share how they answered the question, *As you consider behaviors that brought correction and the opposite postures that brought relationship with God, can you identify any areas in your life where you can pursue the Lord more fully?*
2. Review together the headings from Day Two of the poem found in Isaiah 14:4-23: *The Earth's Reaction to the King's Death, The Underworld's Response, Heaven's Perspective, A Reflection of Life on Earth.* Ask: *What stood out about pride and humility?*
3. Ask women to share their responses to the Day Three Daily Wrap-Up question on page 146.
4. Invite someone to read Isaiah 57:14-21 and Psalm 103:8-14. Ask women to share what parallels they have experienced between responding to God's correction and peace.
5. Ask which metaphor stood out to them from Isaiah 11. Direct a volunteer to read Isaiah 12:1-2 and allow women to share how these verses encourage them regarding the future.

REVIEW

Review the Big Idea for each of the five days of study. Ask for final thoughts or questions regarding the study of God's correction from Isaiah this week.

PRAYER REQUESTS

Allow each woman a chance to share a prayer request. Then instruct the group to silently lift up the requests of the woman on her right in prayer.

TRUST *God's* COMING

SESSION SEVEN

I can't believe we've come to the last week in our study of Isaiah! This week we'll get some glimpses into Christ's return to motivate us toward holy living in the present. The prophet reminds us that while the world often feels out of whack, the best is yet to come. He'll show us some practical postures like prayer and praise that we can exercise as we wait for the future perfection Jesus will bring. Isaiah will also help us assess next steps to take when we feel stuck in our doubts and questions, and he'll help us learn to live with eternity in view. He won't paint everything as rosy, though. We close out our study with a reminder that judgment awaits those who don't believe in Jesus. I pray this will motivate us to cling to the gospel and not let anyone we love slip into eternity unwarned or unprayed for!

MEMORY VERSE

For since the world began,
no ear has heard
and no eye has seen
a God like you,
who works for those
who wait for him!

ISAIAH 64:4

Day One

THE BEST IS YET TO COME

SCRIPTURE FOCUS

Isaiah 60; 61

BIG IDEA

We can trust that Jesus will return and put an end to our earthly suffering.

My husband and I learned an important lesson from a trip he planned for our five-year wedding anniversary. He packed for me, drove us to the airport, and didn't tell me any details about the trip. I would love to tell you that it was awesome, but I hate surprises! I prefer knowing the itinerary ahead of time. My husband absolutely adores surprises so he assumed I would as well, but for me it's all about anticipation and appropriate expectations. The trip to Chicago where we first met was great, but because I thought we were headed for a beach I couldn't hide my disappointment. He and I delight in different aspects of future events—I love knowing a few details, while he loves the mystery of the unknown.

Do you relate more to me or my husband in this story? Think about something you are looking forward to in the next year. Do you feel good about the level of details you know (or lack thereof)?

Whether you have a trip, graduation, milestone birthday, or new season of life on the horizon, thinking about fun in the future can help us through dreary days. As we focus on the return of Christ in our study this week, we will find that we can get excited about the details revealed in prophecy and embrace the mystery of future surprises. We can trust God for a hopeful future believing that Jesus will return and put an end to our suffering.

LIGHT IN THE DARKNESS

I know Jesus is going to come back, but I find it challenging to keep that perspective at the forefront of my mind. Disappointments and difficulties regularly threaten my positive outlook. I love how Isaiah began this last section of his book with a call to remember the bright future the Lord has in store for His followers.

READ ISAIAH 60:1-3. Write down some repeated words from these verses:

Maybe you wrote *rise, shine, light,* or *glory*. In the last seven chapters of Isaiah, we find the word *glory* many times. Darkness can feel like reality for us when we face trials and suffering, but it is not our fundamental reality. Your darkness is temporary, no matter how difficult it feels today. Because you have the promise that God's light and glory will last forever, you can rise and shine above this present darkness.

The glory of the Lord can be a tough concept to wrap our minds around. How would you define "the glory of the Lord" in your own words?

The emphasis on light in the opening verses of Isaiah 60 provides a contrast to the preceding chapter, which stressed the darkness: "We look for light but find only darkness. We look for bright skies but walk in gloom" (Isa. 59:9b).[3]

Unger's Bible Dictionary defines *God's glory* as "the manifestation of His divine attributes and perfections, or such visible splendor as indicates the possession and presence of these . . . God's glory is that in which holiness comes to expression."[1] We began our study of Isaiah with a focus on trusting God's character. Holiness was highlighted in Isaiah's vision of God on His throne (Isa. 6). We also found God's name as the *Holy One of Israel* throughout the pages of Isaiah's book. Glory is the expression of God's holiness. When we are in the presence of God's glory, we will actually experience what we've hoped for in faith. We trust God's coming because He assures us that one day His glory will be tangible.

Scholars often connect Isaiah 60 with John 17 in the New Testament where the theme of "glory" appears repeatedly in Jesus's prayer that the Father would glorify Him so He could glorify the Father.[4]

Pastor Warren Wiersbe said, "When God's glory is on the scene, everything becomes new."[2] What are some recurring challenges in your life that make all things becoming new sound good to you right now?

In many moments I feel contentment and joy, but other times life seems dark. Not every week has something heavy to process, but the darkness can be overwhelming. We've all faced moments in life that left us wondering, *Where is God in this?* Through the prophet Isaiah, God gives us a vision of restoration—a time when all creation will return to its perfect, original state. In Isaiah 60:4-18 we find prophecies of hope regarding a future where:

- People return home with eyes shining and hearts thrilled with joy (vv. 4-5);
- Great wealth from many lands will be brought including offerings for the Lord (vv. 5-7); Ships from the ends of the earth will bring the Israelites home carrying silver and gold (v. 9);
- Foreigners, kings, and the descendants of previous oppressors will come to rebuild towns and serve God's people (vv. 10-16);
- Riches will abound, and peace and righteousness will reign in the land (v. 17);
- Violence and war will disappear, and salvation will surround like city walls (v. 18).

READ ISAIAH 60:20-22. Describe in your own words what will happen in the future.

The Lord will provide light without the sun and moon one day. Revelation gives us more details about this future time:

> And the city has no need of sun or moon, for the
> glory of God illuminates the city, and the Lamb is its light.
> **REVELATION 21:23**

I want to live with hope when I think about this vision of light and restoration. What from Isaiah 60 stands out most to you as something to anticipate?

God's mercy, peace, righteousness, and everlasting light eradicating injustice, difficulty, and darkness sounds incredible to me. Future glory on display reminds us that the best is yet to come—for our lives, yes, but also for the entire world. Isaiah continued into the next chapter with a hopeful message, particularly for those experiencing oppression.

HOPE FOR THE HOPELESS

READ ISAIAH 61:1-3. Circle the letter that best answers the question: Who are identified as the recipients of good news, comfort, and freedom?

A. The poor
B. The brokenhearted
C. The captives/prisoners
D. Those who mourn
E. All of the above

What good things can be anticipated?

The Lord also revealed that He would plant His people like great oak trees of right living (v. 3). These verses reassure us that while we suffer and need comfort now, in the future we can anticipate the ashes of our struggles to be transformed into crowns of beauty. We can trust that every trial we are currently experiencing has an expiration date. Thanks to the Gospel of Luke, we know Jesus is the One these verses reference.

READ LUKE 4:16-21 BELOW. Underline Jesus's words after His public reading of Isaiah 61:

> When he came to the village of Nazareth, his boyhood home, he went as usual to the synagogue on the Sabbath and stood up to read the Scriptures. The scroll of Isaiah the prophet was handed to him. He unrolled the scroll and found the place where this was written: "The Spirit of the LORD is upon me, for he has anointed me to bring Good News to the poor. He has sent me to proclaim that captives will be released, that the blind will see, that the oppressed will be set free, and that the time of the LORD's favor has come." He rolled up the scroll, handed it back to the attendant, and sat down. All eyes in the synagogue looked at him intently. Then he began to speak to them. "The Scripture you've just heard has been fulfilled this very day!"
>
> LUKE 4:16-21

Some older commentators have debated whether Isaiah 61 contains a fifth Servant Song because it refers to the Messiah, but most modern scholars do not take this view, asserting only four Servant Songs found in Isaiah 42; 49; 50; and 52–53.[5]

MEMORY VERSE
ACTIVITY

Read Isaiah 64:4 aloud three times. You can find it printed on page 159.

Jesus shared the good news that He was the anticipated Messiah. He didn't beat around the bush when it came to His identity as the restorer of all creation. With His first coming He sacrificed His life as the final payment for sin. Jesus rose again in victory with the promise to return. When He comes again, we will see an even greater fulfillment of Isaiah 61.

READ ISAIAH 61:4-11. List the illustrations Isaiah used to communicate the joy that is coming (vv. 10-11).

Isaiah's descriptions of eternity include pictures of new clothes, a bride and groom dressed and adorned with jewels for their wedding, and a garden in early spring with plants sprouting everywhere. Most people don't haphazardly plan a wedding or plant a garden. The organization is deliberate, so that when the time is right all the details come together to produce something amazing. Only God the Father knows when Jesus will return (Mark 13:32), but His coming has been prearranged. In the meantime, we can trust that Jesus is coming back. And when He does, we will experience His glory and light rather than the suffering and discouragement we often encounter here on earth. Truly, the best is yet to come!

DAILY WRAP-UP

Today we focused on this truth: *We can trust that Jesus will return and put an end to our earthly suffering.* How would you summarize your personal takeaway from today's study?

Day Two

IN THE MEANTIME

Waiting is one of my least favorite things. Recently, a deer hit my minivan. It happened so fast, and at seventy miles an hour the damage was extensive both to the poor deer and my vehicle. As a confessed excessive planner, waiting to hear back from the body shop was painful for me. In the meantime, I was looking at used cars and obsessing over the calendar wondering how I would drive to all the places I needed to go that week—all less than twenty-four hours after my wreck! I knew I needed to wait patiently and just see how things would unfold, but I wanted something productive to *do* in the meantime.

> **What is something you are waiting for right now? How are you handling the waiting?**

SCRIPTURE FOCUS
Isaiah 62; 63:7-14

BIG IDEA
While we wait, we can pray and praise.

Maybe you are anticipating biopsy results, a court decision, a job interview, or a call from an auto shop like I was. My restlessness and impatience were because I was left feeling uncertain about the future— about a car. I want to learn to trust God in the little things like that so I can strengthen my trust muscle with the bigger things in life. When it comes to looking forward to Jesus's return, the Lord instructs us to do something that will help us connect with Him and release control while we are waiting.

Throughout Isaiah we've seen that a relationship with Jesus is more about *being* in His presence than *doing* certain things. This aligns with our focus on striving less and trusting God more. However, today we will discover that there are some things we can do in our waiting that will bolster our trust in God and temper our tendencies toward excessive planning. Isaiah 62 and 63 reveal that right responses to the reality of Jesus's second coming include prayer and praise.

PRAY FOR THE FUTURE

READ ISAIAH 62:1-12 and record below what the prayers of Isaiah in verse 1 and the prayers of the watchmen in verses 6-7 have in common.

Isaiah said he would not stop praying and posted watchmen to pray day and night. Most Christians would agree that prayer is important, yet many of us struggle with a disconnect in what we believe and how we behave when it comes to prayer. A common problem people face is viewing prayer as something to do in desperation—when you want God to do something you desire. Prayer exists to align us to God's will, not to inform Him of ours. Isaiah focused more on God's promises than his own agenda in prayer. Certainly, we can ask God for anything, but we can pray with confidence for God to bring the blessings He promised for the future.

What are some things you have been asking God for lately?

Now consider those same requests framed in this sentence: Lord, Your will be done with _____.

Watchmen would sit up in towers so they could see in every direction.[7] The Hebrew word for *watchman* comes from the word *shamar*, which means "to keep, guard, observe, give heed, to watch for, to wait for."[8]

Prayer allows us to release control and trust God with our present situations as well as our future worries. Sometimes it feels like things aren't moving as fast as we think they should. We live in a culture that insists on getting everything instantly. Emails and texting have sped up the pace of communication. Last night my daughter clicked a few links on her phone and within thirty minutes, a pizza arrived at our door. We've been conditioned to expect quick responses.

When this expectation for instant gratification seeps into our prayer lives, it creates some fundamental problems. Isaiah teaches us to pray like watchmen.[6] Watchmen spent many hours waiting and watching. Isaiah said that those who give the Lord no rest until He completes His work are like watchmen who are looking out in all directions and praying for God to do what He promised. Watchmen (or watchwomen) pray with expectation but leave the timing in the Lord's hands. Jesus also taught that we should never stop asking in prayer.

READ LUKE 11:5-10. Summarize what you learn about prayer from the story Jesus told.

These instructions from Isaiah and Jesus do not mean that begging God will twist His arm into action. But they do challenge us to pray consistently and intentionally. As we pray more, our trust in God is bolstered, which creates a healthy cycle that looks like this:

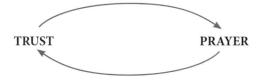

TRUST   **PRAYER**

In the pages of Isaiah, we can see ourselves as watchmen (or watchwomen) who wait and pray with shameless persistence realizing the connection, alignment, trust, and change that can occur through regular communication with God.

PRAISE GOD TODAY

READ ISAIAH 63:7-14. Then fill in the blanks with the three things Isaiah said he would do in verse 7. (Using the NLT Bible version helps with this exercise. Below is Isaiah 63:7 in that version.)

> I will tell of the LORD's unfailing love. I will praise the LORD
> for all he has done. I will rejoice in his great goodness to
> Israel, which he has granted according to his mercy and love.
> ISAIAH 63:7

• I will _____.

• I will _____.

• I will _____.

Isaiah worshiped the Lord while he waited. Worship is about assigning worth and adoration to the Lord, and we can do this in a variety of ways.

What are some ways you worship the Lord?

We can worship God in many ways, including through singing, giving, serving, praying, journaling, silently praising God in our minds, speaking words of praise out loud, and obeying God's commands, just to name a few. Isaiah wrote words of praise to God as the Savior (63:8), Redeemer (63:9), Spirit who "gave them rest" (63:14), and Leader with "a magnificent reputation" (63:14). Praise is an element of prayer that helps us remember God's greatness. Without it, we can begin to see ourselves with big problems and a small God. Worship realigns us to the bigness of our God, which puts our trials into perspective.

Take three minutes to align your behavior with your belief, using one of the choices below:

☐ Listen to a worship song.
☐ Write words of praise in your journal.
☐ Make a list of God's attributes.
☐ Use the alphabet to identify words that describe God.
☐ Other: _____.

Isaiah's prayer and praise hit close to home for me. Impatience is a problem this watchwoman is always on the lookout for. I love that Isaiah shows us some things we can do while we wait, despite any circumstances we face. These verses also give us needed perspective as we wait for Jesus to return.

DAILY WRAP-UP

Today we focused on this truth: *While we wait, we can pray and praise.* How would you summarize your personal takeaway from today's study?

PRAYER

Lord, thank You for prayer. Having direct access to You isn't something I want to take for granted. Make me a watchwoman who is alert and looking around at the signs of our times. Help me to persist in prayer so that I might deepen my trust in You. Come, Lord Jesus! In Jesus's name, amen.

MEMORY VERSE ACTIVITY

Read Isaiah 64:4 aloud one time. Then write it down in your book or on a separate piece of paper.

Day Three

ARE WE THERE YET?

Every time he got in my car this twelve-year-old boy was full of questions. We were doing respite care for another foster family while they were on vacation, and whether we were going on a short errand or a longer drive, he always asked where we were going, how long it would take to get there, and what we would do in the car in the meantime. This happened so many times that I finally assured him he could trust me. He didn't have to know every detail because wherever he went with me—he would be safe. I asked him to trust me with the specifics. All he needed to do was sit back, relax, and enjoy the ride.

SCRIPTURE FOCUS
Isaiah 63:15-19; 64

While I can coach someone else on trusting during a trip, I can't always practice what I preach. I know Jesus is coming back, but I have a lot of questions about when, where, and how He will return, not to mention why it's taking so long! Perhaps you question whether Jesus will return during your lifetime. Or you may wonder how the events of the end times will unfold and how much we should be prepared for these things. We all have questions because of the discrepancy between what we know about God from His Word and our experiences in everyday life.

BIG IDEA
God's silence doesn't indicate His absence.

When the Lord isn't handling things the way we think He should, it can be frustrating. Isaiah sets a great example for us in today's texts, because he wasn't shy about bringing his questions to God. He worked through his doubts and questions with the Lord in order to move from a place of frustration to trust.

When we feel stuck because God doesn't seem to be doing what we think He should, Isaiah reminds us that our conversations with the Lord can be raw and real. In fact, they need to be in order for us to wrestle through the contradictions we encounter as we seek to trust God in a broken world. In Isaiah 63–64, we will discover that Isaiah followed this pattern we can model: (1) complain to the Creator; (2) ask for action; and (3) recognize roles.

COMPLAIN TO THE CREATOR

READ ISAIAH 63:15-19. Write one of Isaiah's complaints in your own words:

References to God as Father are prevalent in the New Testament but very rare in the Old Testament. This is why it's amazing that we find two references to God as Father in Isaiah 63:16 and will encounter another mention of Father in 64:8.

Isaiah asked God to look down from heaven and see. He complained about God's absence in the lives of His people and said, "Sometimes it seems as though we never belonged to you, as though we had never been known as your people" (Isa. 63:19). In some seasons Isaiah felt God's presence strongly—like his vision of heaven in Isaiah 6. But here we find Isaiah in a low moment, complaining about God's silence and asking questions about His lack of intervention. He acknowledged the Lord as "Father" and "Redeemer from ages past" (v. 16), while at the same time admitting that enemies had destroyed the "holy place" (v. 18).

We don't know who else Isaiah shared his frustrations with, but I love it that he brought them to the Lord. I find that when I bring my complaints first to my Creator and work through them in my journal or on my knees in prayer, I am then able to share my feelings with family and friends from a more healthy perspective.

> What current frustrations do you need to bring before the Lord, rather than taking them somewhere else? Take a moment to write a few sentences below telling the Lord how you are feeling about His action or inaction, whether in your life personally or in the world at large.

We can press into our doubts and questions rather than run from them. Being human means having emotions—this means sometimes we feel like God doesn't see us or won't act to help us. After Isaiah's complaints, he then asked God to act.

ASK FOR ACTION

READ ISAIAH 64:1-4. Describe in your own words what Isaiah asked the Lord to do in verse 1.

Most scholars believe Isaiah was referring to the exodus in his request for God to burst down from heaven. The Lord shook a mountain (Ex. 19:16-19) and revealed Himself to His people.[9]

Isaiah asked the Lord to "burst from the heavens and come down" (v. 1). He wanted to see God act in glory and power like He had in the past. Isaiah knew he didn't serve a fake god like those of the surrounding nations. His God is real. The Holy One of Israel parted the Red Sea (Ex. 14:21), held back the rain for forty days (1 Kings 17:1), and made city walls fall to the ground (Josh. 6:20). So, Isaiah asked God to do it again—to act in his own day—to burst down from heaven and intervene.

When we are confused by our circumstances, we can petition God to intervene because He is real. We have seen Him work in our hearts before, and we know He can do it again. He invites us to ask Him for help and trust Him to do what He says He will do in His Word.

Write a few sentences asking God to act in your heart, mind, or circumstances.

The apostle Paul quoted part of Isaiah 64:4 (our memory verse this week) to remind the church that God still acts on behalf of those who wait for Him (1 Cor. 2:9).

Even though Isaiah felt at one point like his people had never belonged to God, he asked God to come and show Himself real again. He acknowledged his doubts but leaned into his faith. These postures of complaining (to our Creator) and asking (for God to act) can help us move spiritually toward greater trust in God. When God seems silent in our lives, remember He is never absent. When He feels far away, ask Him to reveal Himself to you again.

READ ISAIAH 64:5-12. Summarize the roles of God and humans below. (Hint: There are no "right" answers, so use your own words to describe Isaiah's insights.)

People are characterized by _____ (vv. 5-7).

God is _____ (v. 8).

I hope you noticed the three references to sin associated with people in these verses. They may strive to do good, but their deeds are like filthy rags (Isa. 64:6). The Lord is our Father who provides, protects, and disciplines us. He is also the Potter, the one in control to mold and shape us into His design.

As the clay, we are prone to sin and don't always have a clear picture of the master plan. This is why it is so important that we remember God is our Potter, and we can trust Him to mold us and guide us in the way we need to be. Understanding this relationship allows us to trust God's promises. He will burst down from heaven at just the right time. I may think it should be today, but He knows best.

Knowing that Isaiah felt the freedom to bring his complaints and questions to God reminds us that we can be brutally honest in our prayers and bold in our petitions. God's sovereign hand is at work in our lives and our world, even when we don't feel it.

MEMORY VERSE ACTIVITY

Write down Isaiah 64:4. Also record one thought you have as you read over this verse.

DAILY WRAP-UP

Today we focused on this truth: *God's silence doesn't indicate His absence.* How would you summarize your personal takeaway from today's study?

Day Four
ANOTHER TIME, ANOTHER PLACE

Today I had a conversation with myself after my alarm went off. If I stayed in bed and skipped my morning exercise class, then I could sleep an extra hour and my muscles (sore from yesterday's class) could get a break. I tried to discern whether rest or movement would be the right choice for the day, so I asked my current self what my future self would say was best. With a groan, I threw back the covers and headed to the gym. Turns out my future self was right; it felt good to stretch, move, and connect with my workout buddies before tackling the day.

> **What's a choice (big or small) that you've made recently where you considered future consequences in making your decision?**

SCRIPTURE FOCUS
Isaiah 65

BIG IDEA
God promises us more than just this life.

We often evaluate the future impact as part of our decision-making process. This is important to do in our walk with God, too. Thankfully, the Bible provides us with important details about the future so that we can make holy choices as we prepare for Christ's return. This week our focus has been on trusting God's promises about Jesus's return, but that day often feels so far into the future that it doesn't impact my current decisions. Reading through prophetic passages—like the one we will cover in Isaiah today—can feel disconnected from our day-to-day lives. But through God's revealed glimpses of the future, we can live with the end in mind. Doing so helps us focus our attention on eternal things (like trust, love, God's Word, and people) rather than temporal concerns.

In the final pages of his vision, Isaiah wrote about the future. In Isaiah 65, God answered the lament written by Isaiah on behalf of the people of Israel (Isa. 63–64) with a word of hope for their future—the joy of eternity in His presence.

OUR CURRENT STATE

READ ISAIAH 65:1-16. What are a few of the ways the Lord said the people of Israel had provoked Him (vv. 3-7)?

List a few of the blessings the Lord described for His servants, the remnant of His people who would seek Him (vv. 8-16).

"'The Valley of Achor' was the place where Achan was stoned to death because he disobeyed the Lord (Josh. 7). When the Lord restores His estranged wife, Israel, the Valley of Achor will become for them 'a door of hope' (Hos. 2:15)."[10]

In Isaiah 65, God spoke to the nation's blind spots. He allowed their doubts and questions but wanted them to understand how they contributed to His judgment. The Israelites asked why God wasn't intervening in their circumstances to ease their suffering. The Lord explained how they had provoked Him to anger. However, God also acknowledged that not everyone had resorted to human striving.

The Lord illustrated this principle with a description of grapes that shouldn't be destroyed because they still had some good in them. This good wasn't characterized by superior life performance or religious rituals but an attitude of seeking God (Isa. 65:8-10). After addressing the people's lament, the Lord revealed spiritual realities that will take place in the future.

OUR FUTURE REALITY

READ ISAIAH 65:17-25. Draw lines to connect each circumstance below to identify whether each one is a current or future event.

- A new heaven and new earth exist.
- Former things won't be remembered.
- The sound of weeping and crying.
- A baby dies after only a few days of life.
- An old man who dies at one hundred will be considered a youth.
- The wolf and lamb will feed together.

CURRENT

FUTURE

Isaiah reminded his readers that another time is coming in the future that won't be like our time. Most scholars identify this period as the eternal kingdom of Christ (Rev. 21) because in the eternal state, people will not get old and die (Isa. 65:20).[11] We can't know for certain the timeline of these future events or the details of how God will bring about His eternal plan, but we can focus on the future implications of our behavior each day.[12] God has a sovereign plan that will be accomplished, but our decisions matter. As we navigate our days in the meantime, we can seek the Lord and trust Him more, or we can rely on counterfeits and provoke Him with disobedience.

> How does Isaiah's glimpse into the future encourage you spiritually?

Isaiah's descriptions of a future time remind me that this life is not all there is. It stamps eternity in my eyes, which helps me view my blessings and challenges with greater perspective. When I get caught up in the temporary stuff of this life, an eternal lens helps me refocus on what will matter most in the next. My concerns over everything from packed schedules, car repairs, the decisions my kids are making, or scary health news don't overwhelm me as much when I consider them in light of eternity. They must be addressed, but they don't rock my world.

EMBRACING THE IN BETWEEN

Many passages in the New Testament give us further clarity on how we are to live in light of Christ's second coming.

> READ TITUS 2:11-13 in your Bible, and note words or phrases that instruct us how to live as we trust the promise of Jesus's return.

"Oh, that we might know the LORD! Let us press on to know him. He will respond to us as surely as the arrival of dawn or the coming of rains in early spring" (Hos. 6:3).

In light of God's salvation, we are to live lives of repentance, turning from sin and toward the Lord. This is an ongoing posture we take as we desire to seek the Lord and draw near to His heart. God wants His people close, so He reveals Himself and provides clarity about what pleases Him and what doesn't.

Take time now to evaluate your life and ask the Lord to reveal any ways that you can increase your devotion to Him. (Remember that this is not about striving harder but learning to trust Him more.) Record any thoughts that come to mind below:

I need constant reminders of God's good plan for the future because I so easily drift into obsessing over the stuff of this life. I get stuck in the day and need to be awakened to a greater vision of what God is doing. Thinking about God's plan for the future reminds me that my decisions matter. When I stand before the Lord at the end of my earthly life, I know that soccer practice, unloading the dishwasher, and dentist appointments will not seem like proper excuses for failing to seek Him. The Lord offers us the opportunity today to get to know Him more through His Word, through prayer, and through His body, the church. I hope the thought of a future with peace, no tears, and Christ ruling the earth brings a smile to your face and conviction to your heart as you seek to live a life today that honors God.

PRAYER

Lord, help me to remember that I'm not aimlessly wandering through my life. You have a plan. I can hardly wrap my mind around the future when Christ will return to rule on earth. Help me to live in the light of that day—to make decisions that honor You today. Thank You for revealing Your plan to give me hope and strength as I wait for Your perfect timing. In Jesus's name, amen.

MEMORY VERSE ACTIVITY

Attempt to write out Isaiah 64:4 from memory, then check to see how you did.

DAILY WRAP-UP

Today we focused on this truth: *God promises us more than just this life.* How would you summarize your personal takeaway from today's study?

Day Five

HAPPILY EVER AFTER

I love stories that end by resolving the complications of their plot. If I'm going to invest my time in a movie's characters and story, then I want it all to work out in the end. Something in us loves happily ever afters, perhaps because they seldom unfold in our real lives like they do in the movies. The end of Isaiah won't leave us with a feel-good resolution, but it will remind us of the very important reality of God's judgment and hope.

Before we dive into the last chapter of Isaiah, I want to highlight why studying Old Testament prophecy matters. Consider the apostle Peter's words from his second letter:

> We have even greater confidence in the message
> proclaimed by the prophets. You must pay close
> attention to what they wrote, for their words are like
> a lamp shining in a dark place—until the Day dawns,
> and Christ the Morning Star shines in your hearts.
> Above all, you must realize that no prophecy in Scripture
> ever came from the prophet's own understanding,
> or from human initiative. No, those prophets were
> moved by the Holy Spirit, and they spoke from God.
> **2 PETER 1:19b-21**

We did what Peter said to do! We navigated the deep waters of the prophet Isaiah. Peter said the words of prophets are light in a dark place, a metaphor Isaiah used often to encourage trust in the Lord. Many of his prophecies point to Jesus, who is "the light of the world" (John 8:12).

Today, we will not find specific Messianic references, but we will highlight this important gospel truth: Jesus makes the difference between eternal life and eternal separation from God. Our forever destination depends on whether we accept or reject His sacrifice for our sins. Forever is a long time, so we want to be clear on how people can spend it with God.

SCRIPTURE FOCUS
Isaiah 66

BIG IDEA
Jesus makes the difference between eternal life and eternal separation from God.

Prophecy helps us:

- Answer questions we have about eternity;

- Keep perspective in our current trials;

- Pursue a life of obedience in light of the future benefits of holy living;

- Deepen our faith in God's trustworthiness;

- Recognize God's relentless love and forgiveness for His creation.

STRIVING LESS

READ ISAIAH 66:1-6. Identify the qualities that please and displease the Lord:

Who will God bless (v. 2)?

Stephen quoted Isaiah 66:1-2 when he shared his testimony before the Jews in Acts 7:48-50. Paul echoed the same words before the philosophers from Athens in Acts 17:24.

Who will God reject (vv. 3-4)?

Throughout the book of Isaiah, we've seen ritualism, hypocrisy, and self-exaltation identified as serious problems. People devised their own way to relate to God. The Lord called to them, but they turned a deaf ear to His instructions in favor of their own plans. They strived more and trusted less.

This challenge didn't die out with our ancestors. Even after we have committed our lives to Christ, confessing our sin and declaring our need for a Savior, we struggle to stay the course of dependency on the Lord. God is clear in His words through Isaiah: "I will bless those who have humble and contrite hearts, who tremble at my word" (v. 2). The Lord, not me, is to have the first place in my life.

What new insights or experiences have you discovered over the course of our study in the book of Isaiah when it comes to striving less and trusting God more?

TRUSTING MORE

READ ISAIAH 66:7-24. What did the Lord promise to Jerusalem (vv. 12-13)?

How will the Lord punish the world (vv. 15-16)?

What did Isaiah foretell will happen in the future (v. 23)?

Now, if I were Isaiah, I would have ended the book at verse 23 with a hopeful word for the future, the happily ever after when everyone will worship the Lord. But Isaiah left a final warning for those who rebel against God:

> And as they go out, they will see the dead bodies of those
> who have rebelled against me. For the worms that devour them
> will never die, and the fire that burns them will never go out.
> All who pass by will view them with utter horror.
> ISAIAH 66:24

The images in this verse are shocking and leave us with a sobering reminder of the eternal plight of those who do not confess with their mouths and believe in their hearts that Jesus is Lord (Rom. 10:9). This reality should motivate us to evaluate our own salvation and to share the gospel with those we know who are far from God.

Each of us has a choice: We can humbly seek God in faith and trust His plan over ours, or we can strive to live in our own strength and follow our own plan. In our modern society, we often speak of the positive benefits of being a Christian but sometimes fail to warn people of the risk of refusing God's invitation. Charles Spurgeon said, "If sinners be damned, at least let them leap to hell over our dead bodies. And if they perish, let them perish with our arms wrapped about our knees, imploring them to stay. If hell must be filled, let it be filled in the teeth of our exertions, and let not one go unwarned and unprayed for."[13] That last phrase grips me—*let not one go unwarned and unprayed for.*

Take a moment to write a short prayer below thanking God that your eternity is secure because of Jesus.

Now write another short prayer for someone far from God whom you don't want to slip into eternity unprayed for.

Verse 24 is not all bad news. If you are in Christ, then Isaiah's final warning is a reminder that God will make good on His promise to eliminate sin and all its effects once and for all. The end of your life can be anticipated with joy knowing that Jesus is the Messiah foretold in the book of Isaiah, and He will keep His promise to return. The New Testament spells it out succinctly:

> Whoever has the Son has life; whoever does
> not have God's Son does not have life.
> **1 JOHN 5:12**

We can't keep Jesus's saving power to ourselves. If we love people, then we will share with them not only the blessings of living for Jesus but also the impending judgment for those who rebel against God by rejecting His Son.

WRAP-UP

Before we end our time together, review what you've learned over the last seven sessions. Read through the key areas of emphasis on the following chart, and record a brief answer to each question.

SESSION	REFLECTION QUESTION	YOUR ANSWER
Introducing Isaiah	How were hope and judgment both included in Isaiah's message?	
Trust God's Character	What character qualities or names for God have stood out to you from your study of Isaiah?	
Trust God's Calendar	How have you trusted the Lord's timing in your life over the course of the study?	
Trust God's Comfort	How have you experienced God's comfort in the pages of Isaiah?	
Trust God's Commands	How have you found peace in following God's instructions recently?	
Trust God's Correction	How have you experienced God's correction, and what benefits have you received from it?	
Trust God's Coming	What is one blessing Isaiah mentioned that you are looking forward to experiencing after Jesus returns?	

PRAYER

Lord, thank You for promising me a happily ever after. I know things certainly aren't perfect in this life, but I'm so grateful it will be different in the next. Until then, please help me to strive less and trust You more. I want to ponder these truths from Isaiah in my mind and heart in the coming weeks. Please let them sink deep so that You may continue Your transforming work in me. In Jesus's name, amen.

MEMORY VERSE ACTIVITY

Write down or say aloud Isaiah 64:4 from memory.

Love tells the truth

Love = acceptence
Hate - other judgement

Session Seven
VIDEO VIEWER GUIDE

To access the video teaching sessions, use the instructions in the back of your Bible study book.

We want to live in the _____ of His coming.

It's a relationship with Jesus that is the _____ and the _____ for all eternity (Isa. 60:1-3,19-20).

Your suffering has an _____ date.

What to do while we wait for His return:

• _____ with God and others (Isa. 62:1; 64:1).

  Anything that drives you to prayer is a _____.

• _____ ourselves (Isa. 61:1-3).

  God gives a crown of beauty for _____.

• _____ wholeheartedly (2 Pet. 3:11-14; 1 Thess. 5:23-24).

WOW: God loves us enough _____

_____

WOE: _____

_____

Compare yourself to J.C.

ACTION STEP: Strive less and trust God more.

Sins
- Pride - an evil snake
Treatment and neglection of the poor

Isaiah 26:4-6
ACT   A - acknowledge your sin
⭐ C - ask God to create a new heart for change road towards
*   T - trust that God will do it (the change)*

Session Seven
GROUP DISCUSSION GUIDE

SHARE: What is something you're looking forward to in the coming year?

WATCH the video "Session Seven: Trust God's Coming" (26:49 minutes) together and follow along with the viewer guide on the previous page.

MEMORY VERSE
Review Isaiah 64:4 and give the group an opportunity to recite it aloud.

VIDEO DISCUSSION
1. *Ask:* What perspective does the promise of Jesus's return provide as you consider any darkness you're currently experiencing?
2. *Discuss:* What are the most helpful practices in your life that help you stay connected to God?

STUDY DISCUSSION
1. Ask someone to read Isaiah 60:1-3 out loud. Discuss together your definitions for "the glory of the Lord" (p. 161) and brainstorm ways a person's life can bring God glory.
2. Encourage women to share how they filled in the blank on page 166 to this sentence: *Lord, Your will be done with _____.* Discuss the connections they have personally experienced between trust and prayer.
3. Review the three key headings for Day Three: *Complain to the Creator, Ask for Action, Recognize Roles.* Share responses to the Daily Wrap-Up question on page 172.
4. Invite someone to read Isaiah 65:17-25. Discuss their answers to the question, *How does Isaiah's glimpse into the future encourage you spiritually?* (p. 175).
5. Ask women to share their responses to this question on page 178: *What new insights or experiences have you discovered over the course of our study in the book of Isaiah when it comes to striving less and trusting God more?*

REVIEW
Review the Big Idea for each of the five days of study. Ask for final thoughts or questions regarding the study of God's coming from Isaiah this week and from the study as a whole. (Or consider having a wrap-up week as a time for celebration and reflection!)

PRAYER REQUESTS
Ask your group to share prayer requests. Then invite a woman you know is comfortable praying out loud to open the prayer time. Give time for anyone who feels comfortable to pray as they feel led. Close the prayer time, being sure to pray for anything not yet covered.

READ THROUGH ISAIAH

SESSION ONE:
INTRODUCING ISAIAH

SESSION TWO: TRUST
GOD'S CHARACTER
□ Day One: Isaiah 1; 2
□ Day Two: Isaiah 3; 4
□ Day Three: Isaiah 5; 6
□ Day Four: Isaiah 7; 8; 9
□ Day Five: Isaiah 10; 11; 12

SESSION THREE: TRUST
GOD'S CALENDAR
□ Day One: Isaiah 13; 14
□ Day Two: Isaiah 15; 16; 17
□ Day Three: Isaiah 18; 19; 20
□ Day Four: Isaiah 21; 22
□ Day Five: Isaiah 23; 24

SESSION FOUR: TRUST
GOD'S COMFORT
□ Day One: Isaiah 25; 26
□ Day Two: Isaiah 27; 28
□ Day Three: Isaiah 29; 30
□ Day Four: Isaiah 31; 32; 33
□ Day Five: Isaiah 34; 35

SESSION FIVE: TRUST
GOD'S COMMANDS
□ Day One: Isaiah 36; 37
□ Day Two: Isaiah 38; 39
□ Day Three: Isaiah 40; 41
□ Day Four: Isaiah 42; 43
□ Day Five: Isaiah 44; 45; 46

SESSION SIX: TRUST
GOD'S CORRECTION
□ Day One: Isaiah 47; 48
□ Day Two: Isaiah 49; 50
□ Day Three: Isaiah 51; 52
□ Day Four: Isaiah 53; 54
□ Day Five: Isaiah 55; 56

SESSION SEVEN: TRUST
GOD'S COMING
□ Day One: Isaiah 57; 58
□ Day Two: Isaiah 59; 60
□ Day Three: Isaiah 61; 62
□ Day Four: Isaiah 63; 64
□ Day Five: Isaiah 65; 66

HOW TO BECOME A CHRISTIAN

Romans 10:17 says, "So faith comes from hearing, that is, hearing the Good News about Christ."

Maybe you've stumbled across new information in this study. Or maybe you've attended church all your life, but something you read here struck you differently than it ever has before. If you have never accepted Christ but would like to, read on to discover how you can become a Christian.

Your heart tends to run from God and rebel against Him. The Bible calls this sin. Romans 3:23 says, "For everyone has sinned; we all fall short of God's glorious standard."

Yet God loves you and wants to save you from sin, to offer you a new life of hope. John 10:10b says, "My purpose is to give them a rich and satisfying life."

To give you this gift of salvation, God made a way through His Son, Jesus Christ. Romans 5:8 says, "But God showed his great love for us by sending Christ to die for us while we were still sinners."

You receive this gift by faith alone. Ephesians 2:8-9 says, "God saved you by his grace when you believed. And you can't take credit for this; it is a gift from God. Salvation is not a reward for the good things we have done, so none of us can boast about it."

Faith is a decision of your heart demonstrated by the actions of your life. Romans 10:9 says, "If you openly declare that Jesus is Lord and believe in your heart that God raised him from the dead, you will be saved."

If you trust that Jesus died for your sins and want to receive new life through Him, pray a prayer similar to the following to express your repentance and faith in Him:

Dear God, I know I am a sinner. I believe Jesus died to forgive me of my sins. I accept Your offer of eternal life. Thank You for forgiving me of all my sins. Thank You for my new life. From this day forward, I will choose to follow You.

If you have trusted Jesus for salvation, please share your decision with your group leader or another Christian friend. If you are not already attending church, find one in which you can worship and grow in your faith. Following Christ's example, ask to be baptized as a public expression of your faith.

ENDNOTES

SESSION ONE

1. Warren W. Wiersbe, *Be Comforted: Feeling Secure in the Arms of God, Old Testament Commentary: Isaiah* (Colorado Springs, CO: David C. Cook, 2009), 125.
2. Ibid.
3. H. B. Charles Jr. "The Test of True Worship," Apr 8, 2019. Available online at https://hbcharlesjr.com.

SESSION TWO

1. John N. Oswalt, *Isaiah, The NIV Application Commentary* (Grand Rapids: Zondervan, 2003), 72.
2. Ibid.
3. Geoffrey W. Grogan, Isaiah-Ezekiel, *The Expositor's Bible Commentary,* Vol. 6. ed. Frank E. Gaebelein (Grand Rapids: Zondervan, 1986), 29.
4. Walter Bruggemann, *Isaiah 1-39* (Louisville: Westminster John Knox Press, 1998), 15.
5. Merrill F. Unger, *The New Unger's Bible Dictionary,* ed. R. K. Harrison, rev. and updated editions (Chicago: Moody Press, 1988), 1137.
6. Ibid., Gaebelein, 13.
7. Geoffrey W. Grogan, "Isaiah," *The Expositor's Bible Commentary: Proverbs–Isaiah, Revised Edition* (Grand Rapids, MI: Zondervan, 2008). Gaebelein, 55.
8. Ibid., Oswalt, 39.
9. "*Qadowsh,*" Strong's: 6918. Accessed online at www.biblestudytools.com.
10. Kay Arthur, *Lord, I Want to Know You* (Colorado Springs: Waterbrook Press, 1992), 55. Also see "The Names of God in the Old Testament" online at www.blueletterbible.org/study/misc/name_god.cfm.
11. Ann Spangler, *The Names of God* (Grand Rapids: Zondervan, 2009), 35.
12. "*Elohim,*" Strong's: H430. Accessed online at blueletterbible.org.
13. "*Yatsar,*" Strong's: 3335. Accessed online at www.biblestudytools.com.
14. J. Alec Motyer, *Isaiah: An Introduction and Commentary, Tyndale Old Testament Commentaries, Vol. 20* (Downers Grove: Intervarsity Press, 1999), 87.
15. John Goldingay, *Isaiah, Understanding the Bible Commentary Series* (Grand Rapids: Baker Books, 2001), 68.
16. Ibid., Oswalt, 140.
17. Ibid., Goldingay, 67.
18. Ibid., Motyer, 99.
19. Ibid., Goldingay, 71.
20. Ibid., Motyer, 102.
21. Ibid., Oswalt, 146.

SESSION THREE

1. Sharon Rusten and E. Michael, *The Complete Book of When & Where in the Bible and throughout History* (Wheaton, IL: Tyndale House Publishers, Inc., 2005.)
2. Ibid., Wiersbe, 109; Ibid., Motyer, 249. See also https://enduringword.com/bible-commentary/2-kings-18/.

Note: Co-regency among kings was a common practice during Isaiah's time. A king would partner with his son in leadership for many years before completely handing over the reins of leadership.

3. Ibid., Wiersbe, 109.
4. Ibid., Motyer, 249.
5. Ibid., Wiersbe, 110; Motyer, 249.
6. Ibid., Wiersbe, 109.
7. Ibid., Wiersbe, 118; Oswalt, 426; Goldingay, 216.
8. Ibid., Wiersbe, 118; Gaebelein, 236.
9. Ibid., Oswalt, 427.
10. Ibid., Wiersbe, 119.
11. Ibid., Oswalt, 422.
12. Ibid., Goldingay, 219–220.
13. Ibid., Motyer, 268.
14. "*Miktab,*" Strong's: 4385. Accessed online at www.biblestudytools.com. Ibid., Oswalt, 428.
15. "586 BC," Ibid., Rusten.
16. Ibid., Gaebelein, 239.
17. Ibid., Motyer, 270–271.
18. Brian Tracy, *Eat that Frog: 21 Great Ways to Stop Procrastinating and Get More Done in Less Time,* (Oakland: Berrett-Koehler Publishers, 2001), 22–23.
19. Ibid., Gaebelein, 274.
20. Ibid., Oswalt, 529.
21. Charles Boutell, *Haydn's Bible Dictionary* (New York: Ward, Lock & Co.: 1883), 67.
22. Ibid., Wiersbe, 144.
23. Ibid., 146.

SESSION FOUR

1. Ibid., Goldingay, 222.
2. Ibid., Gaebelein, 243.
3. Ibid., Motyer, 283.

4. "*Qavah*," Strong's: 6960. Accessed online at www.biblestudytools.com.
5. Trevor Haynes, "Dopamine, Smartphones & You: A battle for your time," Harvard Medical School Blog, May 1, 2018. Accessed online at https://sitn.hms.harvard.edu.
6. Ibid., Oswalt, 465.
7. Ibid., Motyer, 284; Ibid., Oswalt, 459.
8. Ibid., Wiersbe, 134.
9. Ibid., Oswalt, 460.
10. Ibid.
11. Ibid., Gaebelein, 251.
12. "*Towebah*," Strong's: 8441. Accessed online at www.biblestudytools.com.
13. Timothy Keller, *Counterfeit Gods: The Empty Promises of Money, Sex, and Power, and the Only Hope That Matters* (New York: Penguin, 2009), xvii.
14. "*Nacham*," Strong's: 5162. Accessed online at www.biblestudytools.com.
15. Ibid., Gaebelein, 261.
16. Ibid., 264.
17. Ibid., 265
18. Brown, Driver, Briggs, and Gesenius, *The NAS Old Testament Hebrew Lexicon*, "Shuwb," Strong's: 7725. Accessed online at www.biblestudytools.com.
19. "*Gaal*," Strong's: 1350. Accessed online at www.biblestudytools.com.
20. Ibid., Wiersbe, 137.
21. Ibid., Gaebelein, 254.
22. Ibid., Oswalt, 470.
23. Ibid., Unger, 1069.
24. Ibid., Gaebelein, 256.

SESSION FIVE

1. Ibid., Oswalt, 538.
2. Ibid.
3. "*Shama*," Strong's: 8085. Accessed online at www.biblestudytools.com.
4. Isaiah 48 verses: 1,3,5,6,7,8,12,14,16,20
5. *The NIV Application Commentary* by John Oswalt says, "Just because no one had ever gone home from exiles before does not mean it cannot happen" (Grand Rapids: Zondervan, 2003), 537.
6. Motyer, 356.
7. "*Batach*," Strong's: 982. Accessed online at www.biblestudytools.com.
8. "*Shaan*," Strong's: 8172. Accessed online at www.biblestudytools.com.
9. Ibid., Gaebelein, 186.
10. Ibid., Oswalt, 329.
11. Ibid., 335.
12. "*Uwr*," Strong's: 5782. Accessed online at www.biblestudytools.com.
13. Ibid., Oswalt, 588.

SESSION SIX

1. "*Mishpat*," Strong's: 4941. Accessed online at www.biblestudytools.com.
2. Ibid., Oswalt, 472.
3. Ibid., 168.
4. C. S. Lewis, *Mere Christianity*, Book 3, Chapter 8, "The Great Sin," Kindle location 1665.
5. Ibid., Wiersbe, 56.
6. Ibid., Oswalt, 208.
7. Ibid., Gaebelein, 105.
8. Ibid., 106.
9. Ibid., Wiersbe, 56–57.

10. C. S. Lewis, *The Problem of Pain* (San Francisco: Harper Collins, 1940), 91.
11. Ibid., Gaebelein, 183.
12. Walter Bruggemann, *Isaiah 40-66* (Louisville: Westminster John Knox Press, 1998), 182.
13. Ibid., Motyer, 400.
14. Ibid.
15. "*Shalowm*," Strong's: 7965. Accessed online at www.biblestudytools.com.
16. Ibid., Gaebelein, 88.
17. Ibid., Wiersbe, 50.

SESSION SEVEN

1. Ibid., Unger, 479.
2. Ibid., Wiersbe, 181.
3. Ibid., Oswalt, 641.
4. Ibid., 646.
5. Ibid., Gaebelein, 333.
6. Ibid., Motyer, 432.
7. Ibid., Unger, 1297.
8. "*Shamar*," Strong's: 8104. Accessed online at www.biblestudytools.com.
9. Ibid., Gaebelein, 343.
10. Ibid., Wiersbe, 188.
11. Ibid., Wiersbe, 188; Ibid., Oswalt, 689.
12. Ibid., Oswalt, 689.
13. Charles Spurgeon, as quoted in Greg Morse, "Over Our Dead Bodies Embracing the Costs of Warning the Lost" desiringGod.org. Available online at www.desiringgod.org.

VIDEO VIEWER GUIDE ANSWERS

SESSION ONE

Šā'an means to lean on, trust in, support.

Qāvâ means to wait, look for, hope, expect.

Bāṭah means to trust, trust in; to have confidence, to be bold, to be secure.

drift

truth / times

fifth

afflicting / comforting

SESSION TWO

sovereign / surrendered

clarity / character

Maker / Shaper

holy / higher

clarity / character

redeems

WOW: A vision of God reveals that He is sovereign king.

WOE: Clarity about God's character helps us recognize that we need a Savior so that we can be surrendered.

SESSION THREE

truth / timetable

wheel / worry

Word of God / prayer

threat / threatening

wait / wait

WOW: God's timing is perfect.

WOE: We need to get off the mental hamster wheel and trust God's timeline in our lives.

present

SESSION FOUR

weaken / strengthen

eternity

idols

soul / pleasures

comfort / connection

trust

strength

broken

us

WOW: We serve a God who longs to comfort His people.

WOE: Stop turning to the counterfeit comforts, and ask what does it look like to receive God's comfort?

call

SESSION FIVE

hide / heart / heart / habits

lie / lives

worship / worshiper

listen

rely / God

good

WOW: Jesus died for me.

WOE: Jesus called us to come and die to ourselves.

asking

SESSION SIX

welcome / warnings / wise

truth / truce

heartache / hope

pride

good / evil

neglect / poor

character / comfort

pressure points

Jesus

WOW: God loves us enough to correct our course.

WOE: We welcome His warnings.

Acknowledge your sin.

Change. Ask God to create a new heart in you.

Trust that God will do it.

SESSION SEVEN

light

power / prize

expiration

Communicate

gift

Calm

ashes

Commit

WOW: Jesus is coming back.

WOE: We want to live differently in light of that truth.

More Studies from Melissa Spoelstra

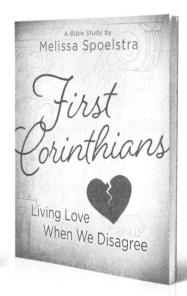

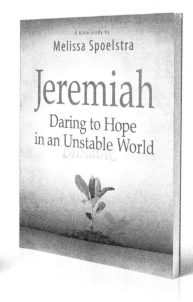

ames of God
's Character Revealed
women study the names of
od, their ideas about God will
ecome more grounded in what
s names tell them, and thus
ore personal, allowing a greater
ust in God to share the details
their lives.

81501878084
rticipant Workbook
81501878107
ader Guide
81501878121
deo Sessions

First Corinthians
Living Love When We Disagree
Explore Paul's first letter to the
Corinthians to learn how we
as Christians are to deal with
differences and divisions—
whether in the workplace, school,
home, social media community,
or church. Discover that the
answer is living and sharing the
radical love of Jesus.

9781501801686
Participant Workbook
9781501801709
Leader Guide
9781501801723
Video Sessions

Jeremiah
*Daring to Hope
in an Unstable World*
In this study, women examine
God's words of instruction to
His wayward people through
the prophet Jeremiah. It
provides six guidelines for
intentional living to overcome
fear, worry, and doubt and put
hope in God alone.

9781426788871
Participant Workbook
9781426788949
Leader Guide
9781426788956
Video Sessions

These and additional Bible studies by Melissa Spoelstra are available wherever books and study resources are sold.

LET'S BE FRIENDS!

BLOG

We're here to help you grow in your faith, develop as a leader, and find encouragement as you go.

lifewaywomen.com

SOCIAL

Find inspiration in the in-between moments of life.

@lifewaywomen

NEWSLETTER

Be the first to hear about new studies, events, giveaways, and more by signing up.

lifeway.com/womensnews

APP

Download the Lifeway Women app for Bible study plans, online study groups, a prayer wall, and more!

 Google Play   App Store

Lifeway women

Get the most from your study.

Customize your Bible study time with a guided experience.

In this study you'll:

- Learn to trust God for who He is and how He reveals Himself in Scripture
- Grow in understanding of the book of Isaiah and its prophecies
- Grasp how Jesus fulfills the promises in the book of Isaiah
- Discover peace in God's commands, character, and comfort

To enrich your study experience, consider the accompanying *Isaiah* video teaching sessions, approximately 25–30 minutes, from Melissa Spoelstra.

STUDYING ON YOUR OWN?

Watch Melissa Spoelstra's teaching sessions, available via redemption code for individual video-streaming access, printed in this Bible study book.

LEADING A GROUP?

Each group member will need an *Isaiah* Bible Study Book, which includes video access. Because all participants will have access to the video content, you can choose to watch the videos outside of your group meeting if desired. Or, if you're watching together and someone misses a group meeting, they'll have the flexibility to catch up! A DVD set is also available to purchase separately if desired.

Browse study formats, a free session sample, video clips, church promotional materials, and more at

lifeway.com/isaiah

HERE'S YOUR VIDEO ACCESS.

To stream *Isaiah* Bible study video teaching sessions, follow these steps:

1. Go to my.lifeway.com/redeem and register or log in to your Lifeway account.

2. Enter this redemption code to gain access to your individual-use video license:

TB3LSKDFJHJG

Once you've entered your personal redemption code, you can stream the video teaching sessions any time from your Digital Media page on my.lifeway.com or watch them via the Lifeway On Demand app on any TV or mobile device via your Lifeway account.

There's no need to enter your code more than once! To watch your streaming videos, just log in to your Lifeway account at my.lifeway.com or watch using the Lifeway On Demand app.

QUESTIONS? WE HAVE ANSWERS!
Visit support.lifeway.com and search "Video Redemption Code" or call our Tech Support Team at 866.627.8553.

FOLLOWING GOD ISN'T ABOUT STRIVING; IT'S ABOUT TRUSTING GOD MORE.

Trust is at the heart of every healthy relationship, especially your relationship with God. It's one thing to say you rest in God, but does your stress level, worry, or general lack of peace give evidence that you rely on Him? In this 7-session study, Melissa Spoelstra encourages you to let go of striving and learn to trust in God's character, His comfort, and even His correction. As you study the book of Isaiah—from the prophet's challenges to the nation of Israel to prophecies of the Messiah—you'll see that you can trust God more than your own human effort or the counterfeits the world suggests.

Lifeway

lifeway.com/isaiah

RELIGION / Biblical Studies / Bible Study Guides

9 781087 750958